VERSAILLES

Text by Claire Constans
Curator of the National Museum
of the Châteaux of Versailles
and Trianon
Translated by Catherine Candea

CONTENTS

THE CHATEAU

THE GARDENS

TRIANON

LES ÉDITIONS D'ART

11, Rue Colbert
78000 VERSAILLES

Marque et présentation déposées 1989

imprimé en France par Mahé — Montreuil

OPENING HOURS

Closed on Mondays
Château : 9 h 45 - 17 h
Grand Trianon : 9 h 45 - 12 h
14 h - 17 h
Small Trianon : 14 h - 17 h
G - Entrance for
groups only
H - Entrance for
the disabled only
J - Access to gardens
• Restaurant -
Tea Room: 39.50.58.62
Telephone
Toilets
1 - Main entrance
Information desk
Cloakroom
Exchange - Audioguides
2 - 3 - Guided Tours
Cloakroom
4 - Guides, Books,
Postcards
5 - The Old Château
6 - The two Ministers' Wings
7 - The *Grand Commun*
8 - The Stables
9 - The King's Apartment
10 - The Queen's Apartment
11 - The Hall of Mirrors
12 - The North and South Wings

FREE VISIT (NON GUIDED)

Entrance 1 : Tuesday to Sunday
The King's Apartment
The Hall of Mirrors
The Queen's Apartment
The other rooms of the museum
are open by rotation
(see Information Desk)

GUIDED TOURS (LED BY GUIDES OF THE NATIONAL MUSEUMS)

Entrance 2 : Tuesday to Friday:
Length: 1 h 30
Individual visitors: 25
14 h 00: The Apartments of the
Dauphin, the Dauphine
and Mesdames
14 h 00: The Apartments of Madame
du Barry and of
Monsieur de Maurepas
15 h 30: The Private Cabinets of the
Queen and the Dauphine
16 h 00: The Château of Versailles
and the Revolution
Entrance 3: Tuesday to Sunday,
9 h 45 - 15 h 30
Individual visitors: 30
The King' Private Apartment and the
Opera
Guided tour (1 h 30)
followed by the free visit of:
The King's Apartment
The Hall of Mirrors
The Queen's Apartment

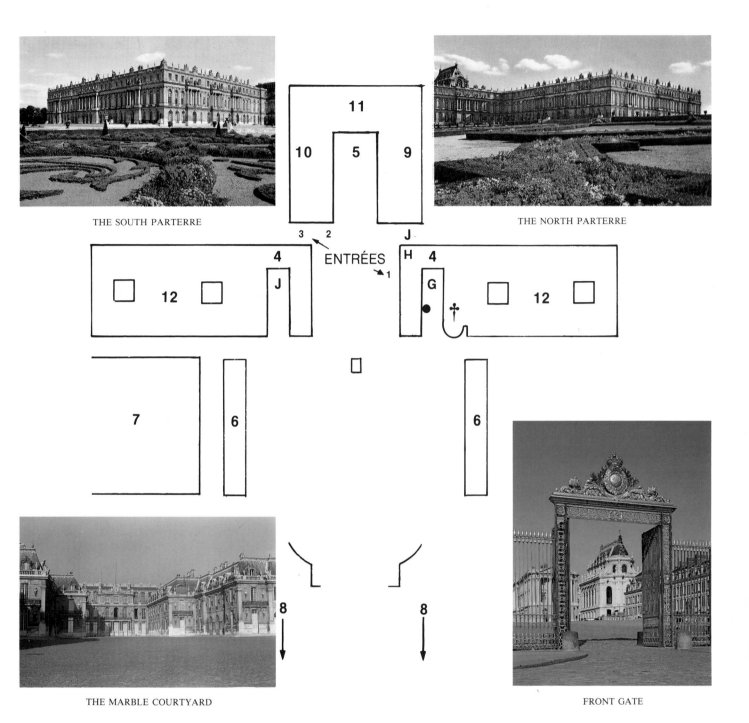

THE SOUTH PARTERRE

THE NORTH PARTERRE

ENTRÉES

THE MARBLE COURTYARD

FRONT GATE

INTRODUCTION

"It is more than a palace, it is a whole town,
Superb in its substance, with splendors of its own
A town? Nay, a world, where of the universe
The eye can behold all the wonders diverse."

Charles Perrault, 1687

Versailles, place of fable and festivity! It was entertainment which made the fortune of this favourite residence of France's hunter kings. It was however love which revealed it, when Louis XIV devoted to Mademoiselle de la Vallière or to Madame de Montespan those sumptuous celebrations that were famous all over Europe Pérain's picturesque costumes are immortalized by the drawings in our archives; the sumptuousness of the ambassadors' receptions by the Royal History stketches; the etiquette, the rivalries and many a familiar scene by the letters and memoirs of the time: Versailles in thus recorded in our memory.

And it remains essentially the same today; great with none of the Louvre's hugeness, it is perfectly balanced by the gardens around which the town of Versailles grew up to be a model to many 18th century capitals, from Leningrad to Washington.

The concern for perfect balance is present everywhere: in the polychrome marble enhanced by gilded bronze and in the painted ceilings; in the art objects whose image is a hundred times reflected by the cabinet mirrors; in the white and gold panelling highlighting the most exquisite inlaid furniture ever. And outside, in the alternation of the bronze bordered pools with the murmuring fountains and the foliages under which marble statues are sheltered.

We should not forget, however, the huge economic effort supporting all this. The masterpieces of the epoch did not have to be imported, for, as Primi Visconti put it: "The best to be found anywhere in the world is now made in France." A whole art of living, of affability, of distance and self-control was developed, which is still regarded as a model of good manners today. For that was the Baroque age. And it is not the least paradox about Versailles that, although often quoted as a perfect example of Classicism, it meant first and foremost light, entertainment, movement, crowd, music, picturesque and performance. The matter was subdued and turned into spirit: this is why it so appeals to the imagination!

CHRONOLOGY

1607 Louis XIII's first hunt in Versailles.
1624 A hunting lodge is built.
1630 Day of the Dupes *(Journée des Dupes)*.
1631 A small château is built to replace the hunting lodge.
1651 Louis XIV's first stay in Versailles.
1661 Death of Cardinal Mazarin; Le Vau begins renovation work.
1663 First Orangery; work begins on the Menagerie.
1664 "Pleasures of the Enchanted Island" with the participation of Molière.
1665 The first statues are put up in the gardens. Grotto of Thetys.
1666 Visit of the Queen of England.
1667 Work begins on the Grand Canal.
1668 "Envelope" by Le Vau; "Great Royal Entertainment" with Molière and Lully. Aix-la-Chapelle Peace.
1670 Building of the Porcelain Trianon; Visit of the Duke of Buckingham. Death of Le Vau.
1671 The "envelope" is completed.
1672 Work begins on the Bath Apartment and on the Ambassadors' Staircase.
1674 24 statues are commissioned for the gardens ("the Grand Commission"). Louis XIV's first lengthy stay. Last great entertainment with the participation of Molière, Lully and Racine.
1677 Louis XIV decides to move to Versailles.
1678 J.H. Mansart begins work on the Hall of Mirrors, Nimègue Peace.
1679 Building of the Ministers' Wings and the Stables.
1680 La Quintinie lays out the King's Vegetable Garden *(Le Potager)*.
1681 The decoration of the State Apartment is completed. The Marly machine. Visit of the ambassadors sent by the Grand Duke of Muscovy.
1682 The King and the Government move to Versailles. Birth of the Duc de Bourgogne.
1683 The first statues of the "Grand Commission" are placed in the North Parterre.
1684 The Hall of Mirrors is completed and the Orangery built.
1685 Work begins on the Colonnade and the North Wing. The King receives the deputies of Alger, the Doge of Genoa and the ambassadors of Muscovy.
1686 Reception of the Siam ambassadors in the Grand Gallery.
1687 Building of the Marble Trianon. Embassy from Muscovy.
1689 The King's silver furniture is melted down. Reception of James II of England.
1699 J.H. Mansart starts work on the Chapel. Embassy from the King of Morocco.
1710 The Chapel is completed, Birth of Louis XV.
1712 Work begins on the Hercules Drawing-Room.
1715 Embassy from Persia, Louis XIV dies. Louis XV moves to Vincennes.
1717 Peter the Great stays in Versailles.
1722 Louis XV moves back to Versailles.
1725 Louis XV weds Marie Lescszinska in Fontainebleau.
1729 The Queen's Bedchamber is redecorated. Audience of the Tripoli ambassadors.
1736 Work is completed on the Hercules Drawing-Room.
1738 Gabriel rearranges the Private Apartment.
1739 Marriage of Madame Elisabeth, Louis XV's eldest daughter, to Infant Don Philip.
1742 Audience of the Ambassador of the "Great Lord".
1743 The State Apartments are refurnished, Building of Saint-Louis Church (now a Cathedral).
1745 Marriage of the Dauphin with the Infanta of Spain (who died in 1746).
1747 Marriage of the Dauphin with Maria Josepha of Saxony. Their apartments are redecorated.
1749 Louis XV's "New Managerie" at Trianon.
1752 The Ambassadors' Staircase is pulled down. Decoration of Madame Adelaïde's Apartment.
1754 Birth of the Duc de Berry, future Louis XVI.
1755 Birth of the Comte de Provence, future Louis XVIII.
1757 Birth of the Comte d'Artois, future Charles X. Damiens attempts to assassinate Louis XV.

1759 Richard and Jussieu create the Botanical Garden of Trianon.
1764 Madame de Pompadour dies.
1768 Marie Lescszinska dies. The Small Trianon is completed.
1769 Madame du Barry moves into the renovated Private Cabinets of the King.
1770 Inauguration of the Royal Opera built by Gabriel: wedding of the Dauphin and Marie-Antoinette. Madame Louise joins the Carmelite order.
1771 Project the rebuilt the façades of the château facing the town (by Gabriel). Work begins on the Louis XV Wing. Marriage of the Comte de Provence to Marie-Joséphine de Savoie.
1773 Marriage of the Comte d'Artois to Marie-Thérèse de Savoie. Birth of the future Louis-Philippe.
1774 The whole park is replanted. Death of Louis XV.
1777 Visit of the Austrian Emperor Joseph II, as Count of Falckenstein.
1778 The Queen's Theatre and Temple of Love by Mique and the English Garden and the Small Trianon. Visit of Benjamin Franklin.
1781 Second visit of Joseph II.
1782 Visit of the Grand Duke (Count of the North) and the Grand Duchess of Russia.
1783 The Queen's Hamlet is built at the Small Trianon. Versailles Treaty sanctioning the independence of the United States.
1784 Pilâtre du Rozier rises in a montgolfier.
1785 The Hamlet is completed. The "necklace affair".
1787 First assembly of the Notables in the *Salle des Menus-Plaisirs*.
1788 Audience of the ambassadors of Tippo-Sahib (Mysore).
1789 Opening session of the States-General in the *Salle des Menus-Plaisirs*. The King, the Government and the Court leave Versailles never to return. Storming of the Bastille. Privileges are abolished. The Declaration of Human and Civil Rights.
1792 The Royal furniture is sold and the works of art are taken to the Louvre.
1793 Louis XVI and Marie-Antoinette are guillotined.
1797 A special Museum of the *Ecole française* is created.
1800 Visit of Pope Pius VII and pontifical blessing from the Grand Gallery.
1806 Restoration work commissioned by Napoleon I, who thinks of taking up residence in Versailles.
1814 Napoleon abdicates. Louis XVIII continues the restoration work.
1833 Louis-Philippe decides to create a museum of French History.
1837 The Museum is inaugurated.
1871 Proclamation of the German Empire in the Hall of Mirrors. The National Assembly sits in the Royal Opera.
1873 Bazaine's trial.
1875 The Hall of Congress is built in the South Wing.
1879 The National Assembly moves back to Paris.
1919 The Treaty of Versailles: end of World War I.
1953 Law on the safeguard of Versailles.
1957 The Royal Opera, entirely restored, is opened to the public.
1962 Debré decree ordering all the objects belonging to the Château and preserved in the French public collections to be brought back to Versailles.
1965 The Grand Trianon is restored and refurnished. It is mainly intended for foreign Heads of State. The 17th Century Rooms are reopened.
1970 The Consulate and Empire Rooms are opened to the public.
1975 Reconstitution of the Queen's Bedchamber and of Madame de Maintenon's Apartment.
1978 *Loi-programme* concerning the restauration of the buildings and décors.
1980 Reconstitution of the King's Bedchamber and of the Hall of Mirrors.
1984 The Staircase designed by Gabriel is built.
1986 Restoration of the Lower Gallery and the Princes' Apartments on the ground floor of the main building.

National Domain of Versailles

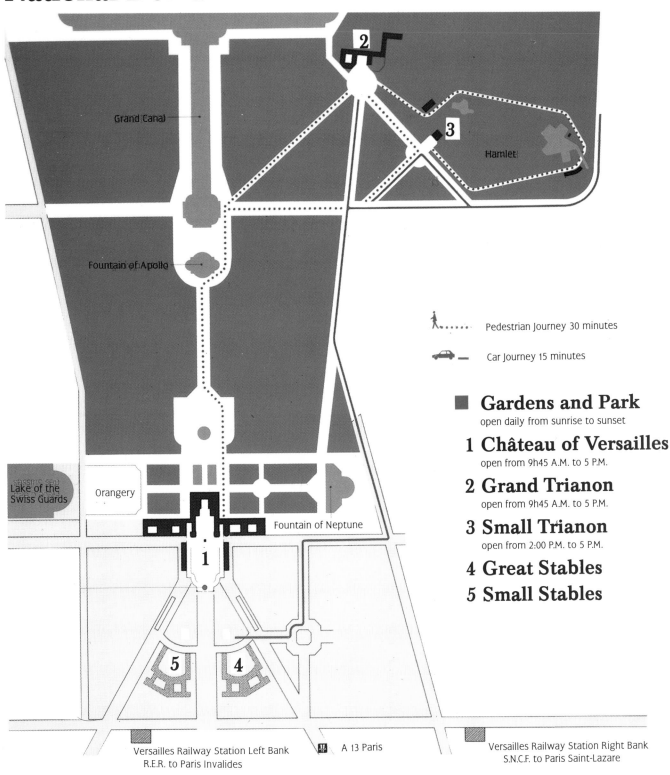

Grand Canal

Fountain of Apollo

Lake of the Swiss Guards

Orangery

Fountain of Neptune

Hamlet

2

3

1

5   4

Pedestrian Journey 30 minutes

Car Journey 15 minutes

Gardens and Park
open daily from sunrise to sunset

1 Château of Versailles
open from 9h45 A.M. to 5 P.M.

2 Grand Trianon
open from 9h45 A.M. to 5 P.M.

3 Small Trianon
open from 2:00 P.M. to 5 P.M.

4 Great Stables

5 Small Stables

Versailles Railway Station Left Bank
R.E.R. to Paris Invalides

A 13 Paris

Versailles Railway Station Right Bank
S.N.C.F. to Paris Saint-Lazare

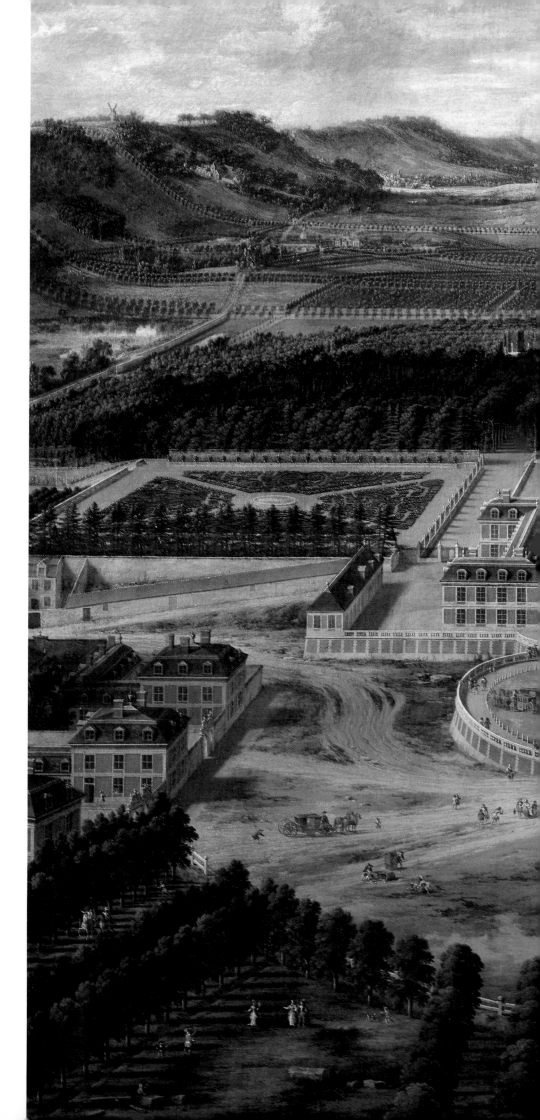

"A little château of cards"

Starting with the Middle Ages, the kings of France often changed their residence within Paris itself and elsewhere in the realm, Wars, the economic frailty of certain areas and the political necessity for the Sovereign to show himself to his people sometimes caused them to settle a long way off: the Loire châteaux are the most beautiful examples of temporary residences. Henry IV turned Paris back into a royal capital but went hunting in Fontainebleau. His successors, all open air sportsmen like himself, went there as well as to Saint Germain and then to Versailles, a true hunting paradise. The Court followed them, which required a complex installation.

Historical notes : 1607, Louis XIII's first hunt in Versailles; 1623, stone mason Nicolas Huau is commissioned to build a little manor of brick and stone; 9th March 1624, Louis XIII sleeps there; 1631-1634, the château is rebuilt and enlarged by Philibert Le Roy; 1651, first visit of Louis XIV; 1663, Le Vau builds two wings at the front of the outbuildings, Le Nôtre sketches the Grand Perspective of the park and the main axes and draws the first flowerbeds and groves (the Maze). Le Vau builds a menagerie and an orangery to the South; May 1664, entertainment with the theme "Pleasures of the Enchanted Island"; 1665, the Grotto of Thetys is built.

VERSAILLES IN 1668, BY PATEL ▷

"This sort of royal beauty"

Louis XIV enjoyed Versailles from the very beginning. At first, he contented himself with the brick, stone and slate château of his father (who had been dreaming of retiring there once his son achieved majority) and enlarged it eastwards by adding pavilions and wings to shelter the annexes (kitchens and stables). The palace was still rarely lived in but the King, the Queen, the Grande Mademoiselle and other members of the Royal family had their private suites next to the Chapel and, later on, to the Billiard Room. At that point, it was a "country seat". But the King grew increasingly attached to it and started a new campaign of "colour" reconstruction towards what was to become the town; then, in 1670, when the whole of Europe resounded with

the name of Versailles, with its celebrations, its fountains and its Thetys Grotto, Louis XIV decided to enlarge the part of the château facing the gardens with a stone "envelope" whose columns, statues and ancient orders make it utterly different in its majesty from the picturesque oriental façade. At the same time, the town grew up around the three wide avenues converging on the château and new essential annexes were built; the *Grand Commun* for the kitchens, the Grand and Lesser Stables and various other outbuildings.

Historical notes : 1668, Louis XIV decides to enlarge the palace on the garden side and offers a "Great Royal Entertainment" at Court; 1669, Le Vau and

d'Orbay are commissioned to carry out the extension work; 1670, Le Vau builds the "stone envelope"; the Porcelain Trianon is built; 1672, the Ministers'Wings at the front of the palace are built; work begins on the King's Staircase and the Bathroom; decoration of the ceilings in the State Apartment; 1678-1684, work in progress on J.H. Mansart's, "Grand Gallery" (decorated by Le Brun) and on the South Wing; 5th May 1682, the Court settles in Versailles; 1684, the King abandons his State Apartment for the apartment overlooking the courtyard; 1685, the North Wing is built; 1687, the Marble Trianon is built; 1710, the Royal Chapel is completed.

△ THE SOUTH PARTERRE

THE FOUNTAIN OF APOLLO AND THE GRAND CANAL, BY P.D. MARTIN ▷

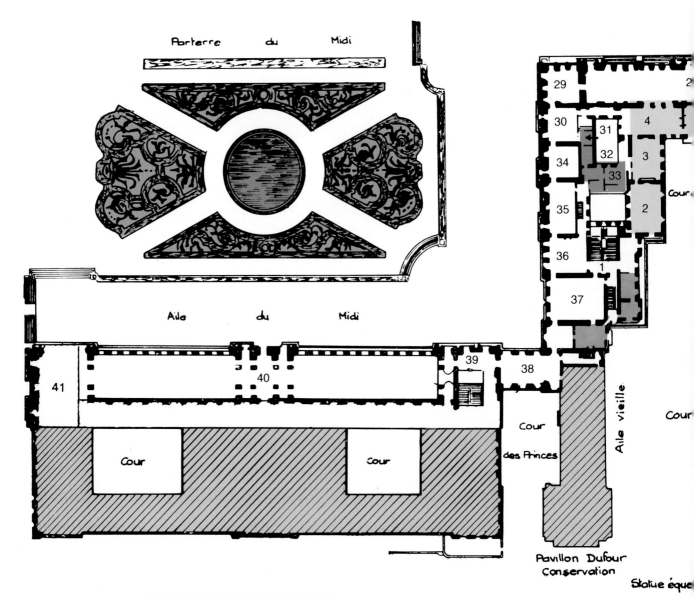

CHATEAU OF VERSAILLES

☐ The King's Suite
  The Royal Opera

■ The Queen's Privy Chamber

▨ The Apartment of Madame de Maintenon
  (Guided Tours)

1 – The Queen's Staircase
2 – The King's Guard Room
3 – The "Grand Couvert"
    Antechamber
4 – The Bull's Eye Window Drawing
    Room
5 – The King's Bedchamber
6 – The Council Chamber
7 – The King's Small Bedchamber
8 – The Clock Drawing-Room
9 – The Cabinet of the Dogs

10 – The King's Staircase
11 – The Dining Room
12 – The King's Study
13 – The Rear Cabinet
14 – The Room of the King's
     Gold Plate
15 – The King's Library
16 – The Porcelain Room
17 – The Billiard Room
18 – The Games Room

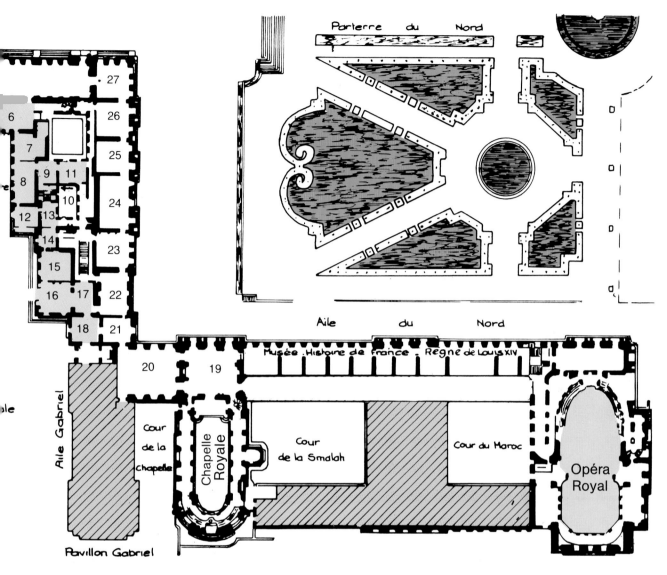

THE FIRST FLOOR LAYOUT

☐ State Apartment and Hall of Mirrors
(Visit at liberty)

19 – The Chapel Drawing-Room
20 – The Hercules Drawing-Room
21 – The Cornucopia Drawing-Room
22 – The Venus Room
23 – The Diana Room
24 – The Mars Room
25 – The Mercury Room
26 – The Apollo Room
27 – The War Drawing-Room
28 – The Hall of Mirrors
29 – The Peace Drawing-Room

30 – The Queen's Bedchamber
31 – The Meridian Cabinet
32 – The Queen's Library
33 – The Queen's Private Cabinet
34 – The Drawing-Room of the
        Nobles
35 – The Queen's Antechamber
36 – The Queen's Guard Room
37 – The Coronation Room
38 – The 1792 Room
39 – The Princes' Staircase
40 – The Battles Gallery
41 – The 1830 Room

The Queen's Staircase

When the State Apartment became public and Louis XIV moved into the apartment overlooking the Marble Courtyard (1684), this staircase became very much frequented; it was the compulsory approach to the apartments of the King, the Queen and Madame de Maintenon, whom the King visited every day for over thirty years.

Historical notes : 1679-1681, the staircase is built by J.H. Mansart; 1701, a loggia is opened on to the Marble Courtyard.
Decoration : multicoloured marble (pilasters of Dinan marble); gilded metal reliefs above the doors by Legros and Massou and niche decoration by the latter; painting by Meusnier (architectural background), Belib de Fontenay (flowers) and Poerson (characters).

THE KING'S FIRST ANTECHAMBER ▷

◁ THE QUEEN'S STAIRCASE

The second Antechamber or the Bull's Eye Room

This was where the courtiers used to wait until it was time for them to enter the King's Bechamber.

Historical notes : 1682, former Bassans Salon (South) and King's Bedchamber (overlooking the Marble Courtyard); 1701, Mansart and Robert de Cotte convert it into its present form.

Decoration: on the ceiling a frieze by Van Cleve, Hurtrelle, Flamen, Poirier, Hardy et Poulletier; pannelling by Dugoulon, Taupin and Le Goupil. – Busts: Louis XIV (Coyzevox) – Paintings: portraits of the Royal family: Marie-Thérèse (Nocret), Monsieur (Mignard), Louis XIV and the Regent on Horseback (Mignard), Mademoiselle de Montpensier (F. de Troy), and Louis XIV's Family (Nocret) represented as Olympian Gods.

THE KING'S SECOND ANTECHAMBER ▷

The King's first antechamber

This is the "room where the King eats", his back to the fireplace, alone, surrounded by his courtiers or, sometimes, with some member of the Royal family: this "Grand Couvert" supper was accompanied by the "King's 24 violins" playing some "symphony for the King's supper" by Delalande. This room was also the meeting point between the people and the Royal authority. Every Monday morning a table and an armchair were brought here "and, after the Council meeting, at about half past twelve, before the King goes down to the chapel to attend mass, if he has not attended it yet, all those who have petitions to bring before the King respectfully lay them on this table. The petitions are all gathered by one of M. de Chamillart's men, who brings the cause list to the King; the King then reads it carefully and writes down in the margin the name of the Minister or of the State Secretary to whom each petition must be sent".

Decoration : 1688-1689, battle paintings by Joseph Parrocel.

The King's Bedchamber

In the centre of the Royal suite, this was first a drawing room opening on the Hall of Mirrors. It was here that the morning ceremony (the *Lever*) took place until the end of the Ancien Régime. At eight o'clock, the King had woken up and received his doctor; a quarter of an hour later the First Gentleman of the Chamber, appointed yearly, told him the important news or asked him some favour; at the same time arrived the *"Grandes Entrées"* who *"may speak to the King"*; at half past eight, the *"Petites Entrées"* attended his toilet (he had his beard trimmed every other day), then the King dressed up. The evening ceremony (the *Coucher*) included the same stages in reverse order with an extra ritual — the King singled someone out by letting him carry the candlestick: "Even though the room was extremely well lit... the King would look around and call out the name of one of the people present, to whom the first valet would give the candlestick. That was a precious favour". It was usually in his bedchamber also that Louis XIV had dinner "au Petit Couvert" (towards one o'clock in the afternoon).

Historical notes: 1668, the King's Grand Drawing-Room; 1682, the room where the King dresses; 1701, the King's Bedchamber; 1761, the two fireplaces are installed; 1980 the original furniture is reconstructed. — **Decoration:** *panelling by Dugoulon, Le Goupil and Taupin; France Watching over the King's Sleep (N. Coustou) —* **Furniture:** *a bed, two armchairs, twelve folding stools upholstered with silk, gold and silver embroidered brocade. The brocade has been rewoven after the winter hangings in Marie-Antoinette's bedchamber, which are very similar to the one made by Lallié for Louis XV. —* **Bust:** *Louis XIV (Coyzevox) —* **Paintings:** *above the doors, Le Marquis de Moncade (Van Dyck), Van Dyck (id.), Saint John Baptist (Carraciolo), Penitent Magdalen (Dominiquin); in the attic, The Evangelists and Caesar's Denier (Valentin), Agar in the Desert (Lanfranc).*

THE KING'S BEDCHAMBER ▷

The Council Chamber

The King used to spend a lot of time in this room. In the morning, to give the orders for the day; after the mass, for the various councils which were held almost every day, even on Sunday but rarely on Friday (State, finances, dispatches, the private council of the Royal Confessor); there were sometimes two councils on the same day. After dinner for private audiences and late at night, after supper, to gather his family around him. When he felt ill, he would have a rest bed taken in there. The paintings by Poussin and Lanfranc, the adorned harpsichord and the gemmed consoles prove that rather than an office or the political centre of France this was the room that the King mostly lived in.

△ FIRST PROMOTION OF THE KNIGHTS OF SAINT LOUIS, BY MAROT

THE COUNCIL CHAMBER △

Historical notes: former Bedchamber and Cabinet of the King; 1684 the King's Cabinet and the "Cabinet des Termes"; 1755 the two rooms are made into the present Council Chamber – **Decoration:** *panelling by Gabriel and Rousseau; above the door, The Story of Minerva by Houasse –* **Furniture:** *the table on which the Versailles Treaty was signed in 1919; the clock commissioned by Louis XV; the Sèvres vases commissioned by Louis XVI. –* **Cabinet:** *brocade satin rewoven after the original made for Louis XV. –* **Busts:** *Scipion, Alexander (dressed by Girardon).*

THE KING'S NEW BEDCHAMBER △

The King's Private Apartment

The sumptuousness of the State Apartment drove the King towards other rooms, easier to live in. The numerous changes that were made in this suite until the Revolution echo the changes in tastes; Louis XIV's Art Cabinet; the Small Gallery decorated by Mignard and so luxurious that its tortoiseshell panelling was never completed; the apartment of Madame de Montespan and then of Madame Adelaïde, daughter of Louis XV. The billiard games, the concerts, the games and the hunters' suppers evoked by the tables which are now displayed in this suite; the exhibition of the finest Sèvres porcelain pieces in the Dining Room, or Porcelain Room (thus called because of the porcelain plaques representing Royal hunting scenes): all this brings out a more familiar aspect of Court life. The simple white panelling with magnificent gilded sculptures shows the extent to which refinement prevailed over sumptuousness at the end of the 17th century. It was in this suite that Louis XV and his grandson slept; it was here also that they worked: the former worked out his skilful diplomacy in his *Arrière Cabinet;* at the time of the "necklace affair", it was in the King's Apartment that the latter decided to have the Cardinal de Rohan arrested.

RIGAUD: LOUIS XV △

17

The Clock Cabinet

Historical notes: *1692 Antechamber and part of Louis XIV's Art Cabinet; 1738, converted into an oval shaped drawing-room; 1760, remodelled into its present form. -* ***Decoration:*** *panelling by Verberckt and Rousseau; above the doors, paintings representing Diane's story (copies after Boucher); the Versailles meridian is embodied by a copper rod inlaid into the floor. -* ***Furniture:*** *astronomic clock made by Passement and offered to Louis XV by the Academy of Sciences (1750) - it is adorned with Caffieri bronzes and its calculations are so accurate "that they do not deviate by one degree in several thousand years"; hunting tables ordered by Louis XV from Slodtz, Foliot and Roumier. -* ***Equestrian statues:*** *Louis XV (scaled down copy by Vassé after Bouchardon's statue which stood in the Louis XV square, now Place de la Concorde), Frederic II (Sèvres bisque).*

The After-Hunt Dining Room

Historical notes: *1692, the King' Bathroom and petit degré; 1750, converted into a dining-room. -* ***Furniture:*** *regulator by Berthou; "study" clock from Louis XIV's Bedchamber in Saint-Cloud - Cabinet: rewoven crimson silk upholstery.*

The Dog's Antechamber

Historical notes: *1692, the King's petit degré; 1738, Antechamber to the Private Apartment -* ***Decoration:*** *panelling designed by Mansart and coming from Louis XIV's Billiard Room (1684); cornice with hunting themes -* ***Cabinet:*** *crimson silk curtains rewoven after the original -* ***Paintings:*** *by Blin, Fontenay and Monnoyer, some of which were commissioned by Louis XIV for Marly.*

ROYAL HUNT (AFTER OUDRY) △

The Private Cabinet

This room became less and less private over the years; it was here that the marriage certificates were signed and it was here also that the "necklace affair" broke out in 1785, when Louis XVI told Cardinal de Rohan: "You shall be arrested!"

*Historical notes: Billiard Room; 1692, part of the Art Cabinet; 1738, converted into a "cabinet à pans" (a room with cut off corners); 1760, final changes. - **Decoration:** panelling by Verberckt (1753) and Rousseau (1760); Louis XVIII cornice - **Furniture:** medal cabinet by Gaudreaux, designed by the Slodtz (1739); corner cupboards by Oeben and Riesener (1760-1769); chairs by Foliot (1774), candelabra commemorating the American War of Independence by Thomire (1783) and Sevres vases commissioned by Louis XVI; pendulum by Roque commissioned by Louis XV (1770); andirons by Thomire (1785).*

◁ THE KING'S PRIVATE CABINET

MEDAL CABINET: BY GAUDREAUX △

The Back (or Arrière) *Cabinet* was a room "used by His Majesty as a retreat, a room where he keeps his papers and where he writes, draws, gives orders and receives dispatches".

*Historical notes: about 1682, oval drawing-room; 1752, dressing-room and cabinet de chaise fitted in; 1760 shelving installed. - **Furniture:** Louis XVI's watch cabinet by Riesener.*

The Cabinet of the Gold Plates

This was where Beaumarchais taught Madame Adelaïde to play music and to sing. Mozart is said to have played here before the Royal family in 1764.

*Historical notes: Madame de Montespan's Apartment; Small Gallery; 1753 Madame Adelaïde's Gilded Cabinet; 1769, redecorated by Gabriel - **Decoration:** panelling by Verberckt; medal cabinet by Benneman decorated with butterfly wings (1774); porcelain plaques after Van Loo.*

THE CABINET
◁ OF THE GOLD PLATES

The Dining Room of the "New Rooms"

1769, decoration of the Dining Room; panelling by Verberckt. Above the door: *Metamorphosis of the Gods* by Collin de Vermont. "Sky blue" cabinet. Louis XV commissioned a series of "Royal hunting scenes" from the great Jean-Baptiste Oudry. Louis XVI had them copied out on porcelain plaques, featuring himself instead of his grandfather. The plaques were hung in the Dining Room of the New Rooms.

Louis XVI's Library

*Historical notes: Madame de Montespan's Apartment; central part of the Small Gallery; 1753, Madame Adelaïde's Bedchamber; 1769, Louis XV's Games Room; 1774, Gabriel converted it into the library it is now. - **Decoration:** pannelling by Antoine Rousseau; book bindings on the doors by Fournier; fireplace by Bizot and Gouthière, formerly decorating Madame de Barry's Drawing Room at Fontainebleau and used here again by Louis XVI - **Original furniture:** Reisener table. Benneman commode and sphinx clock by Juhel, formerly in the bedchamber of the Comte de Provence; Sené furniture from the King's suite in Compiègne - Cabinet of "painted pekin", reconstructed according to the documents of the epoch.*

THE KING'S LIBRARY △

◁ THE DINING ROOM OF THE "NEW ROOMS'"

The Games Room

Owing to extensive purchase and restoration of the silk upholstery, the furniture of this room has been almost completely reconstructed. This partly compensates the lost sumptuousness of Louis XIV's Rare Objects Cabinet, full of works of art, gems, "vases of gold, diamond and agate inlaid with emeralds, turquoises, jade, pearls, etc.", through which the King liked to escort his guests himself.

Historical notes: Louis XIV's Rare Objects Cabinet; 1753, Madame Adelaïde's First Antechamber; 1775 redecoration - Furniture: corner cupboards by Riesener (1774); chairs by Boulard (1785) - Cabinet of rewoven crimson and gold brocade; Savonnerie carpet woven for the Grand Gallery of the Louvre.

LOUIS XIV'S GAMES ROOM △

THE BATTLE OF MONS, BY VAN BLARENBERGHE △

THE ROYAL OPERA ▷

The Royal Opera

Lully and Molière had to content themselves with the Marble Courtyard and with improvised theatres put up in the gardens; Racine was confined to Madame de Montespan's Apartment; Madame de Pompadour occupied the Ambassadors' Staircase; the Grand Stables themselves were requisitioned: what a shame for the music, the comedy and the ballet that were so dear to the Kings!

In 1768, Louis XV decided to carry out Mansart's great plan for an opera house at the far end of the North Wing and he commissioned Jacques-Ange Gabriel to do it. The plan was elliptic and the stage of ample proportions. The interior being of wood, it was fast and

not to expensive to build and had excellent acoustic. Moreover, the machinist Arnoult provided the means to turn the Opera Hall into a ball room or banquet hall: jacks would be used to bring the stalls up to the level of the stage, to lower the circle floor and to cover the orchestra pit. The whole interior is done in trompe l'œil: mirrors, false marble, false lapis lazuli, false gilded bronze - all made in Durameau's workshop. The stucco decorations, particularly abundand in the foyer, were made by Pajou and his team. The columns, pilasters and low relief recall Mansart's decorations a century before.

MAIN EVENTS:

16th May 1770, banquet to celebrate the marriage of the Dauphin with Marie Antoinette. 17th May, *Perseus* by Lully; 19th May, full dress ball.

1st October 1789, banquet offered by Louis XVI's bodyguards to the troups that had been summoned to Paris on the first signs of revolutionary unrest.

10th June 1837, Meyerbeer's *Robert le Diable,* played before Louis-Philippe and 1500 guests on the inauguration of the Museum of History.

25th August 1855, dinner in honour of Queen Victoria.

1871: the Opera house is assigned to the French National Assembly and then to the Senate.

1957, opening after restoration.

THE ROYAL OPERA (STAGE END) △

VIEW ON THE ROYAL BOX (DETAIL) ▷

26

Music in Versailles

Music was everywhere in Versailles: in the Chapel, where the King daily attended mass and often the *Salut* accompanied by motets, choirs, strings, wind instruments and organ; in the Mars Drawing Room, where symphonies alternated with lyric dramas and Court airs and where the hapsichord was more and more frequently heard; in the open air where trumpets' blows announced the arrival of coaches, princely cortèges or embassies.

The King commissioned the Italian Lully, whose **Atys** had won him over, to renew the French music; for his Chapel he chose Delalande because his music ''pleased him''. Later on, Louis XV had the honour (of which he was obviously unaware) of having young Mozart at his ''Grand Couvert'' dinner: the boy ''sat by the Queen so as to speak to her constantly, to make her laugh and kiss her hands...'' It was the time of the ''Querelle des Bouffons'': the ''Queen's corner'' was all for the Italian opera bouffe and the ''King's corner'' all for the French opera.

Marie Antoinette played music and she did it well. She was also a composer. She patronized Gluck but often wondered at the keen, typically Parisian quarrels, which sometimes sounded almost like a religious war.

Some of the beautiful old musical instruments can still be seen in Versailles: the Chapel organ; Madame Adelaïde's violin and a small organ which probably belonged to her as well; two hapsichords, one by Ruckers and the other one by Blanchet; two pianofortes having belonged to Empress Marie-Louise, one (by Taskin) in the Small Trianon and the other one (by Erard) in the Grand Trianon.

THE MARQUIS DE SOURCHES: FAMILY, BY DROUAIS △

HARPSICHORD DECORATION ▷

The Royal Chapel

"He was very respectful of the Church. During mass, everybody had to kneel down at *Sanctus* and remain so until the priest's communion for, if he came to hear the slightest noise or to see people whisper during mass, he was highly displeased."

Yet this good Christian King took a long time to build a house for God! Little is known about the first three chapels of the château apart from Le Brun's magnificent plans which, had they been carried out, would have given a Baroque vigour to the French painting and decoration. The fourth chapel stood on the present site of the Hercules Drawing Room. The fifth and final one displays the sumptuousness and serenity of the end of Louis XIV's reign.

Many ceremonies were celebrated here: its consecration in 1710, the presentation of the gold rose to Marie Lescszinska in 1736, all the princely marriages subsequently registered in the parish records.

Historical notes: 1699-1710, the Chapel is built by H. Hardouin-Mansart and R. de Cotte, of white Creteil stone; about 1750, Chapel of the Sacred Heart (Sacré Cœur), behind the altar, by Gabriel; on the left, the Chapels of Saint Louis and of the Virgin are superposed. -
Ground floor: polychrome marble floor bearing the arms of the Kings of France; carved wall decorations, based on the parallel between the Old and New Testament (Vassé, Coustou,

Le Lorrain...): Vassé: Pietà and the Adoration *in the altar; side altars built under Louis XV and decorated by the Adam brothers, Bouchardon, Jouvenet, La Patte, the Slodtz and Verberckt - Lower vestibule: on the site of the Grotto of Thetys; Coustou: The Crossing of the Rhine (which Louis XIV had intended for the War Drawing Room). - Upper Chapel Vestibule: ceiling paintings by Jouvenet (Whitsun, above the Royal gallery), Coypel (God the Father, in the nave), La Fosse (Resur-* *rection, in the apse) and the Boullognes (Apostles, in the side galleries); organ loft by Cliquot and Tribuot, designed by R. de Cotte and carved by Dugoulon, Le Goupil and Taupin; Savonnerie Carpet (1760) - Drawing Room: Corinthian columns and pillars foreshadowing the Chapel decorations; arcades adorned with the Christian virtues by Coustou, Lapierre, Poirier and Poulletier; Vassé: Glory Holding Louis XV's Medallion; Bousseau: Royal Magnanimity.*

THE MAIN ALTAR △
◁ THE ROYAL CHAPEL

THE CHAPEL VESTIBULE △

The Hercules Drawing-Room

This large salon (18 m/60 ft × 14m/45 ft) was intended by Louis XIV as a setting for Veronese's masterpiece *Meal at the House of Simon*. Another painting by Veronese, *Elieze and Rebecca*, was subsequently hung on the opposite wall. Sumptuously decorated, this last room of the State Apartment was the perfect setting for the festivities of the 18th century. Among the most famous ones were the Full Dress Ball of 1739, the Grand Couvert for the wedding of the Duc de Chartres in 1769, the one given for the Dauphin's birth in 1782, the extraordinary audience of the ambassadors of Tippo Sahib, Sultan of Mysore, in 1788 and the presentation of the deputies of the Estates-General to the King on 2nd May 1789.

The ceiling was decorated by François Lemoyne (1736) and the result pleased the King so much that he appointed the artist his First Painter (the latter, however, was to commit suicide shortly after). Above the cornice, the coving is decorated with four Virtues (*Justice, Fortitude, Constancy, Courage*) separated by Cupids pointing to the Labours of Hercules. In the centre, *Hercules Standing in his Chariot* arrives at the Olympus, where Jupiter gives him his daughter Hebe in marriage as a reward for his labours. Mars and Vulcan are contemplating the fall of the vices and demons. Apollo is sitting on the steps of the Temple of Memory, much like Louis XIV used to sit on the throne step, watching the games and the dancers or listening to music.

*Historical notes: site of the fourth chapel; 1710-1730, decoration by Robert de Cotte - **Decoration:** Claude Tarlé, rare polycrome marble (Sarancolin, Antin, Rance); Vassé, fireplace bronzes; Veronese, The Meal at the House of Simon (1570-1576), given to the King by the Republic of Venice in 1664 (frame by Verbeckt) and Elieze and Rebecca.*

THE HERCULES DRAWING-ROOM △

30

MEAL AT THE HOUSE OF SIMON, BY VÉRONÈSE △   CEILING (DETAIL), BY LEMOYNE ▽

The State Apartments

"Madam, there shall be an apartment and you shall dance there. We are no ordinary people; we must devote ourselves entirely to the public." The King was thus sermoning the recalcitrant mourning Dauphine. The King was a public character. He was born and he died in public, for he belonged to his country. His subjects could easily come near him, provided they were dressed properly, but this public life required some organization. Saint-Simon spoke about the "mechanism" of a life that is so minutely regulated that anywhere in the kingdom, anybody provided with a compass and a watch can tell what the King is doing. The State Apartment was particularly crowded in the morning, when the King crossed it on his way to the Chapel and on the

to the Chapel and on the three "Apartment" evenings a week when the guests, whom the King informally joined, would crowd around the buffets and the refreshments, play card games or billiard and dance. His successors tended to spend their leisure time in the more intimate setting of their Private Apartment.

The Queen, could use her Apartment as she wished, except for the *Grand Couvert* which she had together with the King. She was even given the Peace Drawing-Room, where the "Queen's games" took place and where Louis XV was sometimes known to fill up his wife's purse.

LOUIS XIV RECEIVES THE PERSIAN AMBASSADOR, BY COYPEL △   THE ABUNDANCE DRAWING-ROOM ▷

The Abundance Drawing-Room

The decoration of the ceiling depicts some of the objects belonging to Louis XIV's Cabinet of Rare Objects (behind the Abundance Drawing-Room), many of which are now in the Louvre.

The Royal collections are far from being a vain word. Louis XIV watched out for paintings, sculptures and rare objects with sometimes unseemly anxiety; he supported young artists and paid them a pension to make copies after the masterpieces in Rome; he understood that it was a sovereign's duty to protect art and so he commissioned a large number of works. One cannot ignore, on the other hand, the part played in the 18th century by Madame de Pompadour or Madame du Barry in the evolution of art, particularly in the field of decorative arts.

*Historical notes: vestibule of Louis XIV's Cabinet of Rare Objects - **Decoration**: ceiling, Royal Munificence (Houasse); above the door, Abundance (Audran); portraits, Philippe V, the Grand Dauphin and the Duc de Bourgogne (Rigaud); Louis XV (J.B. van Loo); bronze busts and porphyry vases from the Royal collections. Inlaid medal cabinets after designs by Boulle. Genoan velvet gallooned with a gold fringe, woven after an ancient model.*

CEILING OF THE ABUNDANCE DRAWING-ROOM, BY HOUASSE ▷

The Venus Drawing-Room

On "Apartment" evenings, light refreshments, jams, candied or fresh fruit were served out of the baskets and basins displayed around the room: "everyone took and chose what was most to his taste".

*Historical notes: upper vestibule to the Ambassador's Staircase. - False perspectives and trompe l'œil statues of Meleager and Atalanta (Rousseau) - **Ceiling** (Houasse): Venus Subjugating the Gods and Powers; between the corner paintings of Jupiter Raping Europe and Amphritrite: Titus and Berenice, Anthony and Cleopatra, Jason and Medea, Theseus and Ariadne; in the covings: Augustus Presiding over the Circus Games, Nebuchadnezzor and Semiramis Ordering the Gardens of Babylon to be Erected, Wedding of Alexander and Roxana, Cyrus Taking up Arms to Save a Princess. These compositions are framed by* Rapes *and* Chases: *Pan and Syrinx, Apollo and Daphne, Neptune and Coronis, Saturn and Cybele.*

Against the marble panelling designed by Le Brun, antique busts and statue of Louis XIV by Jean Warin (1672).

THE VENUS DRAWING-ROOM △

THE AMBASSADORS' STAIRCASE (A MODEL) ▷

The Ambassadors' Staircase

The decoration of the Ambassadors' Staircase was designed by Le Brun at the same time as the plans for the State Apartment. Of Italian inspiration, it was panelled with marble and trompe l'œil columns, niches and capitals of gilded bronze. An almost avant-garde zenithal opening was framed by the months, the Muses, the parts of the world, the main heroic deeds of Louis XIV's early reign and several episodes of the Greco-Roman Antiquity. These sumptuous decorations were continued in the Venus and Diana Drawing-Rooms.

This staircase was seldom used as it was reserved for ceremonial entrances and ambassadors' retinues, which would then pass through the State Apartment to reach the Hall of Mirrors. It was pulled down in 1752, during the rearrangement of the King's Private Apartment.

CEILING OF THE VENUS DRAWING-ROOM, BY HOUASSE ▷

The Diana Drawing-Room

Historical notes: *upper vestibule to the Ambassadors' Staircase -* **Ceiling** *(Blanchard): Diana Presiding over Hunting and Navigation -* **Covings** *(Audran): Cyrus Hunting the Boar, Caesar Sending a Roman Colony to Carthage; (La Fosse) Jason and the Argonauts Landing in Colchyda; Alexander Hunting the Lion.* **Above the doors** *(Blanchard): Diana and Acteon, Diana Protecting Arethusa, (offertory of flowers and sacrifice) -* **Antique busts** *(Capitoline Venus and Woman Wearing a Tiara) from the collection that Cardinal Mazarin had bequeathed to Louis XIV; bust of Louis XIV by Bernini (1665) - Low-relief depicting the Flight to Egypt, set into the chimney-piece.*

◁ LOUIS XIV, BY BERTIN

THE AMBASSADORS' STAIRCASE (A MODEL) ▽

The Mars Drawing-Room

Historical notes: *Guard Room; 1684 Games Room, Ball Room or Concert Hall; 1750, removal of the musicians' galleries on either side of the fireplace -* **Ceiling:** *Mars on his Chariot (Audran) between Hercules Supporting Victory (Jouvenet) and Terror, Fear and Dread (Houasse) -* **Covings:** *Caesar Reviewing his Legions and Demetrios Poliorcetes Attacking a Town (Audran); Cyrus Haranguing his Troops and Albinus (Jouvenet); Constantin's Triumph and Alexander Severus Degrading an Officer (Houasse); corner low relief by the Marsy brothers -* **Above the doors:** *Justice, Fortitude, Temperance, Prudence by Vouet, from the Château of Saint-Germain. The Family of Darius at Alexander's Feet by Le Brun (1660); The Pilgrims of Emmaus, after Veronese; David Playing the Harp, by Domenichino; Marie Lecszinska by C. van Loo (1747); Louis XV by L. M. van Loo (1746).*

The Mercury Drawing-Room

Historical notes: the King's Ante-chamber; 1682, Bedchamber; 1700, Philip V's chamber; 1715 and 1774, chapel of rest for Louis XIV and Louis XV - **Ceiling and covings** *by J.B. Champaigne: Mercury on his Chariot Drawn by Two Cocks; Alexander Receiving an Indian Embassy; Ptolemy Conversing with the Scholars; Alexander Sending Animals to Aristotle; in the corners: The Dexterity of the Body, The Knowledge of the Fine Arts, Justice and Royal Authority - Above the doors: Apollo and Daphne (A. Coypel) and Acis and Galathea (Michel Corneille), commissioned by Louis XIV for the Trianon. -* **Furniture:** *automaton clock presented to Louis XIV by Morand (1706); commodes by C.A. Boulle from Louis XIV's bedchamber in Trianon (1709); Gobelins tapestry: Conference with Cardinal Chigi (1665-1680).*

CEILING OF THE MERCURY
DRAWING-ROOM, BY CHAMPAIGNE ▷

THE MARS DRAWING-ROOM △

HE MERCURY DRAWING-ROOM ▷

The Apollo Drawing-Room

Historical notes: *the King's Bedchamber; 1682 Throne Room. - **Ceiling** by La Fosse: Apollo in his Chariot Drawn by Four Horses; **Covings:** Veturia Begging her Son Coriolan to Raise the Siege of Rome; Vespasian Ordering the Coliseum to be Erected; Augustus Ordering the Construction of the Misene Port; Porus and Alexander; in the corners, the four ends of the world - **On the walls:** Louis XIV (Rigaud, 1701), Louis XVI (Callet);*

Above the doors: *The Birth of the Dauphin (Blanchard, 1663), Fame Carrying Glory to the Four Corners of the Earth (Bonnemer, 1666) - **Furniture:** Candelabra of gilded wood made by Bable and Foliot (after Gondouin) for the Hall of Mirrors (1769); the gold threaded tapestry is an allegory of fire (17th century).*

◁ THE APOLLO DRAWING-ROOM

THE DOGE OF GENOVA MAKES AMENDS TO LOUIS XIV, BY HALLE △

The War
Drawing-Room

Historical notes: Jupiter Draw-ing-Room (King's State Cabinet); 1678, construction by Mansart and Le Brun - Dome: France Triumphant surrounded by The Defeat of Germany, The Defeat of Holland, The Defeat of Spain and by Bellona Bringing Rebellion and Discord (Ch. Le Brun). - Decoration: polychrome marble panelling and gilded bronze trophies by Buirette and Lespingola; chimney-piece designed by Le Brun and carved by Coysevox: Louis XIV's Victory over the Ennemies of France and Clio Writing the History of the King; two busts of Roman Emperors, which were saved from the Tuileries fire in 1871.

The Hall
of Mirrors

Historical notes: 1678-1684, built by Mansart and Le Brun on the site of Le Vau's terrace - Decoration of marble with "French order" capitals (cock, radiant Apollo and fleur-de-lis); on the walls and cornices, gilded bronze trophies by Coysevox, Tubi, Le Gros, Clérion, Flamen; in the niches, Bacchus, Urania, Modesty, Venus in Modesty, antiques from Louis XIV's collections.

THE WAR DRAWING-ROOM ▷

Ceiling: *decoration by Le Brun; the large paintings evoke the war with Holland (1672-1678) and the medallions and trompe l'œil paintings the War of Devolution (1667-1668) as well as the great administrative reforms of Louis XIV's early reign. -* **Furniture:** *two of the four alabaster covered tables come from* the collection of the duc d'Antin; the antique vases and busts come from Royal collections; the 1770 chandeliers and candelabra were reconstructed in 1980 after the originals and the archive documents.

◁ THE HALL OF MIRRORS

The Peace Drawing-Room

Historical notes: *the Queen's Grand Cabinet; 1678, cf. War Drawing Room; 1792 the Queen's Games Room, separated from the Hall of Mirrors by a partition. - **Ceiling:** paintings by Le Brun: the Apotheosis of France surrounded by Spain, Christian Europe, Germany and Holland at Peace - On the walls, same decorations as in the War Drawing Room; antique busts; Lemoyne's Louis XV Bestowing Peace on Europe (1729), andirons by Boizot and Thomire (1786).*

Versailles is not only a residence but also the façade of the realm. Etiquette, precedence, beauty — all this contributed to its magnificence as did the fabulous silver furniture which had to be melted down in 1689 for the King to pay his military contributions.

The Queen's Bedchamber

This is the main room in the Queen's Apartment. Marie-Thérèse, Marie Leszczinka and Marie-Antoinette all lived here and so did the Dauphines. As for the King's Bedchamber, its restoration, which took thirty years, involved research as well as long and delicate reconstruction work; restoring the wainscoting; identifying the "white brocade Tours silk with flowers, lily roses and others, with most effective interlacing ribbons and peacock tails, the whole framed by superb, richly fringed green edgings..."; tracking down, the bedspread and the andirons in private collections; carving the balustrade after a drawing of the one in the Parade Room of the Palais Royal, which in its turn was similar to the model chosen by Marie Lescszinka; providentially purchasing the original wall clock made in 1745 and placed in the bedchamber by Marie-Antoinette.

Historical notes: designed for Marie-Thérèse; 1730, panelling by Dugoulon, Le Goupil and Taupin after Robert de Cotte; 1734, creation of the paintings above the doors: Youth and Virtue Introducing Two Princesses to France (Natoire) and Glory Taking Possession of the Children of France (Troy); 1735 piers by Gabriel and ceiling by Boucher (Charity, Abundance, Fidelity, Prudence); 1770, the arms of France and Austria carved by Rousseau in the archings; 1775, tapestry portraits of Joseph II and Marie-Thérèse by Cozette - Original furniture (restored to what it was in 1789); Schwerdfeger's jewellery cabinet (1786), andirons by Boizot and Thomire (1786), the Baillou and Crescent wall clock (1745), Sené's chimney-piece (1786) and the bedspread by Desfarges (1786) - Replacement furniture: armchairs by Tilliard and folding stools from the suite of the Comtesse d'Artois in Versailles; balustrade, Savonnerie carpet and reconstructed summer cabinet (brocade Tours silk with flowers).

THE QUEEN'S BEDCHAMBER ▷

△ THE MERIDIAN CABINET

THE LIBRARY △

The Queen's Private Cabinets

From the alcove in her Bedchamber the Queen could go into her Private Cabinets − several badly lit rooms on a mezzanine, overlooking the inner courts.

In 1781, the *Meridian* Cabinet, former Oratory of the Duchesse de Bourgogne, was redecorated for the Dauphin's birth by the Rousseau brothers after Mique's drawings: arrow-pierced hearts, dolphins, eagles and garlands of wood and bronze applied onto the mirrors. The table made of

petrified wood comes from the collections of Charles I of England and was offered to Marie-Antoinette by her mother; the blue "grenadière" cabinet is a faithful reproduction. The same taste for an austere style can be noticed in the Library frieze (formely Marie-Thérèse's Oratory, then Marie Leszczinka's painting workshop). The pannelling decorations in the Gold Cabinet (formerly the Duc de Bourgogne's bedchamber) are clearly taken from Antiquity: tripods, burning cassolet-tes, the sphinx, the fireplace caryatids. Oudry's pineapple was placed above the door by Marie-Antoinette as homage to the botanical research work encouraged by Louis XV at the Trianon.

Furniture: commode by Riesener (1779), brought from Marie-Antoinette's Bedchamber in Marly and formerly belonging to the Comtesse d'Artois; Naderman's harp which reminds us of Marie-Antoinette's taste for music.

The Room of the Queen's Gentlemen

This was the room where the Queen received ambassadors and held her circle.

*Historical notes: Queen's Drawing-Room; 1785 redecorated by Richard Mique - **Ceiling:** paintings by Michel Corneille: Mercury Spreading his Influence over the Arts surrounded by Penelope, Sapho, Aspasia, and Cerisene - **On the walls:** mythological paintings by Boucher and tapestry portrait of Louis XV by Cozette; above the doors: Pygmalion and Dibutade, by Regnault; fireplace with bronze ornaments by Gouthière - **Furniture:** commodes and corner cupboards (Riesener, Gouthière, 1786), candelabra (Daguerre); mantelpiece ornaments of Turkish influence.*

The Queen's Antechamber

It was here that the King and the Queen dined in public *("au grand couvert"),* turning their backs to the fireplace and facing the musicians' gallery. In the 18th century, the atmosphere of these dinners was one of conviviality, which allowed the King or the Queen to address any person attending the ceremony.

*Historical notes: formerly Room of the Queen's Guard; 1680, antechamber sometimes used as theatre - **Ceiling:** arching paintings by Vignon and Paillet, illustrating royal virtues through portraits of ancient heroines (Rodogune, Cybele, Arpelia, Zenobia, Ipsicarte, Clelia) - Portraits of Louis XVI's three aunts by Madame Labille-Guiard (1787); above the doors, paintings by Madeleine de Boulogne (1675).*

Marie-Antoinette

Marie-Antoinette (1755-1793), Archiduchess of Austria, married the Dauphin, future Louis XVI in 1770. They had four children: Madame Royale (who became Duchesse d'Angoulême by marrying her cousin, the son of the Comte d'Artois), Louis (the Dauphin, who died in 1789), the Duc de Normandie (Louis XVII who died in the Temple, in 1795) and Madame Sophie (who died as a child).

She doesn't seem to have been fully happy in a Court which was not always favourably disposed towards her (Maurepas; the Cardinal de Rohan who tarnished her name in the "necklace affair" because of which, though innocent, she was given the nickname of Madame *Déficit*). Her youth, her sense of festivity and her taste for music left many traces in Versailles. The decorations of the Queen's Apartment, the arrangement of her Private Cabinets and of the Small Trianon, the building of the Hamlet or the Trianon Theatre all express the "gentle way of life" at the end of the Ancien Régime.

The Room of the Queen's Guard

Historical notes: 1672, Chapel; 1676-1681, final redecoration - Paintings by Noël Coypel, from the Jupiter Drawing-Room: the history of Jupiter and "great deeds" evoking the King's equity; Ptolemy Philadelphus Setting the Jews Free, Solon Explaining His Laws, Trajan Dispensing Justice, Alexander Severus Distributing the Wheat to the Poor; marble panelling enhanced by gilded bronze (Le Gros, Massou), designed by Le Brun.

◁ MARIE-ANTOINETTE AND HER CHILDREN, BY E. VIGÉE-LEBRUN

THE ROOM OF THE QUEEN'S GUARD △

THE MUSEUM OF FRENCH HISTORY

The 19th century in Europe was marked by the arousal of national consciousness; the Revolution spread out the ideas of the Enlightenment and the rulers sought recognition in history. Louis-Philippe, a constitutional King, created thus a museum devoted to "All the Glories of France", in order to show the historical events leading to the 1830 Revolution, which had brought him to the throne, as well as some of the major undertakings (particularly Colonial ones) of his reign. He therefore wholly covered the walls with paintings and sculptures coming from former Royal or Imperial collections to which he added reproductions and new works he had commissioned himself. The finest pieces can still be seen today: the Crusade Room, the Room of the States General, the Coronation Room, the 1792 Room, the Empire Room and the Hall of Battles.

The Coronation Room

*Historical notes: 1676, Chapel; 1682, Guard Room; 1833, completly redecorated by Nepveu - **Ceiling**: The 18th Brumaire (Callet, 1806); in the covings, allegories and inscriptions of Directoire and Consulate victories. - **Above the doors**: Virtues (Gérard) - On the walls: Bonaparte Consul, then Emperor, Joséphine and Marie-Louise; The Coronation (David, second version of the Louvre painting, 1808-1822), The Battle of Aboukir (Gros, 1807), commissioned by Murat for his palace in Naples; The Army Taking the Oath and The Distribution of the Eagle Standards (1810), commissioned by Napoleon for the Tuileries.*

THE CORONATION ROOM ▷

The 1792 Room

Formerly Room of the Merchants under Louis XV and of the Swiss Guards under Louis XVI. Within his museum of "all the Glories of France", Louis-Philippe dedicated this room to the year of the declaration of "the country in danger" (by Cogniet) and to the first great revolutionary victories: Valmy and Jemmapes. At the side of Dumouriez, Kellermann, La Fayette, the Duc de Chartres (future Louis-Philippe), Rochambeau and Bonaparte, Lieutenant Colonel in the 1st Corsican battalion, are the lower rank officers, many of whom were to become Marshals of the Empire.

The Hall of Battles

1833: built on the site of apartments of the King's children and siblings. Created by the architects Fontaine and Nepveu and the decorator Plantar, it is continued by a room dedicated to the July Monarchy (1830). Its zenithal lighting evokes Hubert Robert's plans for the Grand Gallery of the Louvre.

The 120m (394 ft) long walls lined up with 33 paintings, 82 busts and 16 bronze tables illustrate the history of France from Tolbiac (496) to Wagram (1809) such as Louis Philippe wanted the French people to remember it. At a time when history was growing into a science, when the Chartres School was created and when Chateaubriand, Guizot, Augustin Thierry, Michelet and Prosper Merimée wrote their major works, Louis Philippe's Museum was meant to express the conscience of a people that had very early on become a nation fortified by its rulers' sound administration.

Clovis at **Tolbiac**, Charles Martel at **Poitiers**, Philippe Auguste at **Bouvines**, Jeanne d'Arc at **Orléans**, François I at **Marignan**, Condé at **Rocroi,... Fleurus, Rivoli, Austerlitz**: all these names had become symbols of the century-long fight to safeguard religion and the integrity of the national territory. But as national history sometimes also includes the assistance given to other nations, Louis Philippe commissioned a description of the French participation in the American War of Independence: La Fayette, Rochambeau and Amiral de Grasse surround Washington in **The Battle of Yorktown** (Couder). The moderate descriptive scenes make room for the hero's portrayal. Unlike Gérard or Vernet, Delacroix shows Saint Louis in a storm of iron, blood and colour at the **Battle of Taillebourg.**

▽ THE DEPARTURE OF THE NATIONAL GUARD, BY COGNIET

◁ THE BATTLE OF VALMY, AFTER VERNET

THE HALL OF BATTLES △

Madame de Maintenon's Apartment

Madame de Maintenon's Apartment, in which Louis XIV made a number of important decisions between 1682 and 1715, was recreated in 1975. Special attention should be paid to the passage between the Bedchamber and the Grand Cabinet, which was built according to the King's wish that "there be two doors in the corner, which will open on the passage so that when they are closed... there will be no sign of a door there... and when the doors are open, there will seem to be a wall made on purpose".

The sketches and plans made by Le Brun, Van der Meulen and Jouvenet for the State Apartment and the Chapel were presented here, as well as Cotelle's gouaches representing the gardens as they were in the 17th century.

Madame de Pompadour's Apartment

While their liaison lasted (1745-1750), Louis XV installed Madame de Pompadour in the attic of the State Apartment, which overlooked the North Parterre and the hotel that had been built for her at the Reservoirs. The Bedchamber is still decorated with Verberckt's original pannelling. In 1743, to facilitate the access to the Apartment, Arnoult built a "flying chair" which worked with a counterweight. From 1750 up to her death in 1764, Madame de Pompadour (a Duchess by then) lived on the ground floor.

Madame du Barry's Apartment

This apartment, formerly belonging to Maria-Josepha of Saxony, the Dauphin's widow, was the setting for the suppers during which Louis XV heated the coffee himself on a stove. The Library furniture (sofa designed by Delafosse, parrot cage ornated with porcelain flowers) is indicative of the Countess's taste. The Grand Cabinet and Bedchamber stand on the site of the Small Gallery, which Louis XV had had decorated with "exotic hunting scenes" by Boucher, Lancret, etc., today in the Amiens museum.

The Maurepas Apartment

Offered by Louis XVI to the minister Maurepas (whose portrait by Brenet can still be seen here), this suite of rooms is typical of the apartements granted by Royal favour. The 18th century pieces furnishing it now were bequeathed by the Duke and Duchess of Windsor.

◁ MADAME DE MAINTENON'S APARTMENT
MADAME DU BARRY'S DRAWING-ROOM ▽
◁ MADAME DE POMPADOUR, BY NATTIER

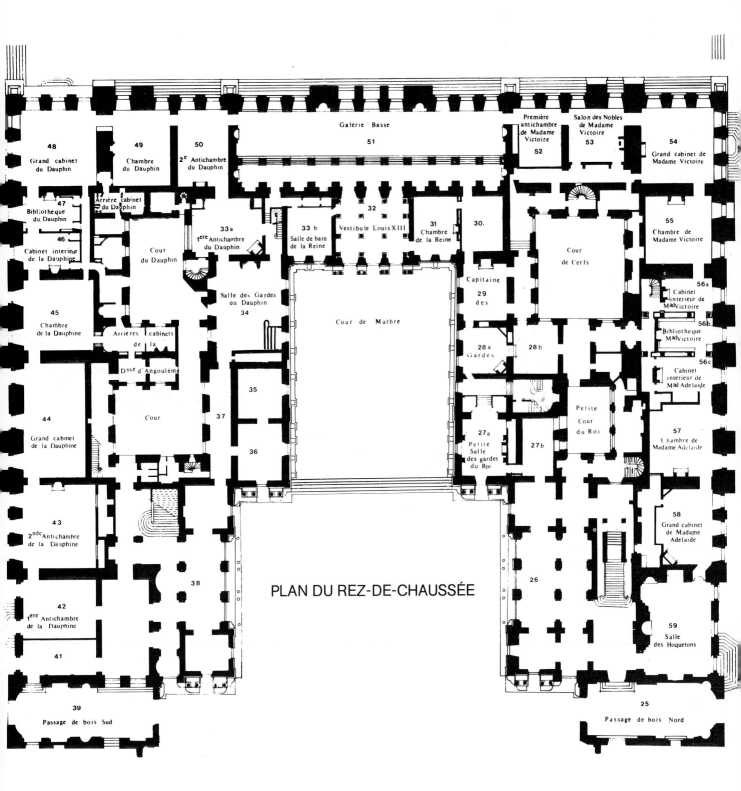

PLAN DU REZ-DE-CHAUSSÉE

THE PRINCES' APARTMENTS

The ground floor of the Château was made up of sumptuous apartments: Louis XIV's Bathchamber, the Apartments of the Duc and Duchesse d'Orléans, the Dauphin, the Dauphine, Louis XV's daughters, Marie-Antoinette, the Captain of the Guard. Some of them have been restored according to the original items of decoration preserved (chimney pieces and panelling) so as to create a suitable setting for the Royal and Princely furniture that the museum has been striving to acquire for about forty years. The paintings by Rigaud, Nattier, Drouais, Vigée-Lebrun evoke not only the successive inhabitants of these rooms — the decorations of which show the 18th century taste for comfort and refinement — but also the main actors of a particularly Europe-centred political life.

The Dauphine's Apartment

The Marquise de Thiange, sister of Madame de Montespan, Monsieur, Monseigneur, la Grande Demoiselle, the High Chaplain of France, the Master of the Wardrobe, the Maréchal de Villars and the Regent each in turn, lived in certain rooms of this Apartment, before it was decorated for Maria-Josepha of Saxony, the Dauphin's second wife (1747). It was then occupied by the future King Louis XVI until his marriage, by his brother, the Comte de Provence and finally by Madame Royale and the first Dauphin.

The First Antechamber, standing on the site of the chapel, is dedicated to Louis XV's Accession (portraits by Rigaud and Belle) and to his Coronation in Reims (by P.D. Martin).

The Second Antechamber evokes Louis XV's youth: the portrait of the Infanta *Marie--Anne-Victoire,* once his fiancée (by Belle); a large equestrian portrait of the King by Van Loo and Parrocel (1723); *Peter the Great* (by Nattier) reminiscent of the Tsar's visit to Versailles in 1717; *The Turkish Ambassador Mehemet Effendi Entering the Tuileries* (by Parroucel, 1721).

The Grand Cabinet: *Marie Lescszinska* (by Belle) is flanked by the King and Queen of Poland. *Stanislas Lescszinski* and *Catherine Opalinska* (by J.B. Van Loo); the console was commissioned for this room and the barometer above it was made for the Dauphin, the future Louis XVI.

Bedchamber: the only original pieces of decoration are the paintings above the door: *Psyche* and *Venus* by Restout. Portraits of *Madame Henriette as Flora* and Madame Adelaïde as Diana, by Nattier; bed "à la polonaise"; model of coach made for the Dauphin.

Private Cabinet: the Martin varnished panelling was restored and completed with Oudry's *Seasons* (1749). The Gaudreaux commode and the B.V.R.B. secretaire were made for the first Dauphine in 1745.

THE DAUPHINE'S PRIVATE CABINET △

The Dauphin's Apartment

The Library was the work cabinet of Louis XV's son. Martin's varnished panelling (1755) and the frieze of arabesques and angels are indicative of his taste to the same extent as Vernet's *Four Hours of the Day* (above the door, 1763). The Gaudreaux desk was used by Louis XV and his son; the porcelain top commode made by Criaerd for this room evokes the participation of the King and his son to the Fontenoy battle.

The Grand Cabinet : the panelling was made by Verberckt (1747); the paintings above the doors (by Natoire) come from Marly and from other places in Versailles: *Telemach and Calypso, Bacchus and Ariane, Diana's Rest, Beauty Rekindles Love.* The portraits of Louis XV's daughters (1749) were painted at Fontevrault where they were being brought up. Jacob's furniture comes from Louis XVI's Games Room at Saint-Cloud (1785); the terrestrial and celestial globe (by Mantelle, 1781) was commissioned by Louis XVI for the first Dauphin; the Dauphin's desk was made by B.V.R.B. (1745).

△ THE DAUPHIN'S LIBRARY

◁ THE DAUPHIN'S GRAND CABINET

Bedchamber: formerly the Regent's work cabinet. Panelling by Verberckt (1747) and bronze adorned fireplace by Caffieri. Laquered rose and violetwood bookcase by B.V.R.B. Portraits of *Marie-Thérèse-Raphaelle,* the Dauphin's first wife and of her parents, *Philippe V* and *Elisabeth Farnese* (L.M. Van Loo); *The Farm,* copy by Marie Lescszinska after Oudry.

Antechamber: The second one was Monseigneur's sumptuous "Cabinet de Glaces", decorated with mirrors, rare marquetry and consoles supporting crystals, chinaware and hard stones. Special attention should be paid to the impressive series of portraits of the Royal Family by Nattier: *Marie Leszczynska Wearing a Gown* (1748); *Madame Adelaïde Making a Bow* (1756), *Madame Elisabeth in Hunting Gear.*

The First Antechamber of Madame Victoire reflects the way of life at Court around 1750: portrait of the *Marquis de Marigny,* Madame de Pompadour's brother (Tocqué); *The Cup of Chocolate* (Charpentier), a family portrait of the Comte de Toulouse; Olivier's paintings, which depict the fêtes given by the Prince de Conti on his Ile Adam estate or at the Temple in Paris. This series of paintings is the most precious reference we have about the decoration, the furniture and the costume of the time. Moreover, *Le Thé à l'Anglaise* is one of the rare testimonies of Mozart's visit to Paris in 1766.

THE DAUPHIN'S BEDCHAMBER △

◁ FÊTE GIVEN BY THE PRINCE DE CONTI, BY OLIVIER

Madame Victoire's Apartment

Louis XIV's former Bath Apartment was made into a suite of rooms for the Comte and Comtesse de Toulouse, then for Louis XV's daughters and particularly for Madame Victoire (1769-1789). Portrait of the Marquis de Marigny, the brother of Madame de Pompadour (Tocqué) in the First Antechamber; Fables by La Fontaine (Oudry) in the Second Antechamber; in the State Cabinet, panelling by Verberckt (1763) and Tilliard furniture commissioned for the visit of Gustav III of Sweden to Versailles (1783); in the Bedchamber panelling by Rousseau and corner cupboards by Peridiez (1769). Mesdames' furniture and personal objects in the Private Cabinet and the Library (agate goblets, books, coffee set, desk).

△ MADAME VICTOIRE'S STATE CABINET

◁ MADAME VICTOIRE'S PRIVATE CABINET

Madame Adelaïde's Apartment

Besides Mesdames, this three roomed apartment was occupied by Maria Josepha of Saxony and Madame de Pompadour. The visitor can admire the fine Sené seats commissioned by the Duchesse d'Harcourt (Private Cabinet), the Foliot seats (Bedchamber), an organ and a violin having probably belonged to the most musical of Louis XV's daughters (State Cabinet) as well as the Royal family portraits by Nattier, Van Loo and Drouais.

The Room of Actons (Salle des Hocquetons)

The name under which this Guard room was known comes from the trompe l'œil decoration of trophies and armours, which recall the duties of the Château guards (1672).

MADAME ADELAÏDE'S PRIVATE CABINET ▷

DRAWING-ROOM ORGAN ▽

THE ROOM OF ACTONS ▽

The Apartment of the Captain of the Guards

This strategically situated apartment was the obligatory passage to the King's Private Apartment on the first floor and to his Private Cabinets on the second. It was here also that Damiens attempted to assassinate Louis XV in 1757. The walls are lined with paintings illustrating Court life in the second half of the 18th century: *Marquis de Sourches* (Drouais), *Wedding in Schönbrunn of the future Joseph II*, Marie-Antoinette's brother.

△ THE GROVE OF APOLLO'S BATHS, BY H. ROBERT

◁ MESDAMES VICTOIRE, SOPHIE AND LOUISE, BY DROUAIS

Louis XV's European policy, life at Court under Louis XV, the support that the latter had granted to the American "insurgents" are all illustrated here by a series of magnificent effigies; *Louis XV* (Drouais, 1774); *The Dauphin as Colonel of the Dauphin-Dragoon Regiment* and *Marigny* (Roslin); *Benedict XIV* (Subleyras); *The Knights of the Holy Ghost Pay Homage to Louis XVI the Day after His Coronation* (Doyen) and portraits of his brothers as knights of the Order (Drouais); *Suffren, Ségur, La Fayette* call to mind the American War of Independence, as do Van Blarenberghe's gouaches representing *The Storming of Yorktown* in 1781.

In the bedchamber, special attention should be paid to Hubert Robert's paintings depicting the replantation of the gardens which Louis XIV ordered as soon as he came to the throne; to Gautier-Dadoty's, portraits of the *Comtesse de Provence*, the *Comtesse d'Artois* and *Marie-Antoinette Playing the Harp in Her State Bedroom* and finally, to Casanova's *The Comte de Saint-Priest's Embassy in Constantinople.*

Besides Louis XVI's beautiful portrait by Duplessis, this room displays the finest array of virtuosity and sensitivity of the late 18th century French painting. The next (and last) room, in which most paintings are the work of Madame Vigée-Lebrun, is almost entirely dedicated to Marie-Antoinette: her portrait "with a rose", several fine Court portraits and a replica of the famous necklace by means of which the tactless Cardinal de Rohan and an adventurous crook, the Comtesse de Lamotte, definitely ruined her reputation in the eyes of the people.

MARIE-ANTOINETTE HOLDING
A ROSE, BY E. VIGÉE-LEBRUN ▷

THE 17th CENTURY ROOMS

The North Wing was built by Mansart in 1686 to house the Princes' Apartments. The ground floor and the first floor are now made up of 23 rooms lined with paintings and sculptures from former Royal collections and seizures of emigrants' property. There are portraits of Henri IV, Louis XIII, Louis XIV, Richelieu, Mazarin, Colbert and all the actors of the Monarchy at its peak; works illustrating events and currents of thought (Protestantism, Jansenism) or the Royal patronage (the Academies); pictures of Royal mansions, wars, fêtes, family celebrations and embassies; and finally a large number of paintings by Champaigne, Beaubrun, Nocret, Vouet, Testelin, Mignard, Le Brun, Van der Meulen, Rigaud or Parrocel. The essential part played by Louis XIV and Colbert can never be emphasized enough.

Not only did the King stimulate trade and economy but he also surrounded himself with scientists and musicians, bestowed pensions on the artists, commissioned "histories" of his reign, which entailed political as well as artistic consideration – particularly within the Academies.

FOUNDATION OF THE OBSERVATORY, BY TESTELIN △

△ MADEMOISELLE DE TOURS, BY MIGNARD

LOUIS XIV AT VINCENNES, BY VAN DER MEULEN ▷

70

From the Revolution to the Restoration

The works relating to the French Revolution are scarce and they are the more important as they bear witness to events that were often distorted by the illustration or propaganda engravings. Some are anonymous, like the *Storming of the Bastille* or the *Storming of the Tuileries*; some are historically marked, like Kucharski's portraits of Marie-Antoinette which was pierced with a pike during the sack of the Tuileries in 1792; some bear the signature of highly distinguished artists like *The Celebration of the National Federation* by Hubert Robert and some are the work of less famous painters like Carteaux's *Louis XVI Wearing the Cockade*.

△ OATH IN THE JEU DE PAUME, BY DAVID

MARAT'S ASSASSINATION, BY DAVID ▷

It is however David who towers over the whole collection, with his drawings, sketches and paintings commissioned by the Revolution. His magnificient incompleted *Oath in the Jeu de Paume* reveals a mixture of Neo-Classical rigour and revolutionary enthusiasm while *Marat's Assassination* uses emotion, silence and compassion to emphasize the greatness of the hero. Both of them were painted as tribute to a new and vigourous truth which is also illustrated by young Charlotte Corday's gesture in a nearby portrait.

BONAPARTE AT THE ARCOLE BRIDGE, BY GROS △

SÈVRES VASE △

◁ MARIE-LOUISE AND THE KING OF ROME, BY GERARD

The imperial Epic

The ground floor of the South Wing as well as the attic and the Chimay Attic are hung with paintings by David' pupils — Gros, Girodet, Guérin, Gérard, etc. — depicting the important moments of the Empire. The epic leads the visitor from Arcole (1796) to the return from Elba (1815), Baron-General Lejeune has a brilliant concern for details (Aboukir, The Pyramids or The Spanish War); Meynier's paintings are austere (Eylan) and David's dramatic (Bonaparte Crossing the Alps) while the portraitists' works reveal their sensibility (Girodet: Belley, Chateaubriand; Danloux: Delille). An exceptional series of portraits by Gérard depicts the society of the time.

THE 19th CENTURY ROOMS

The rooms of the museum that are still being restored are the ones dealing with the French history from the restoration to the interwar period; the Paris revolutions; the European wars of independence; the cultural, artistic and political life; Royal and Imperial families. Out of the large number of painters whose works will be exhibited here, the best represented are Gérard, Vernet and Winterhalter.

LOUIS-PHILIPPE AND HIS SONS, BY VERNET △

75

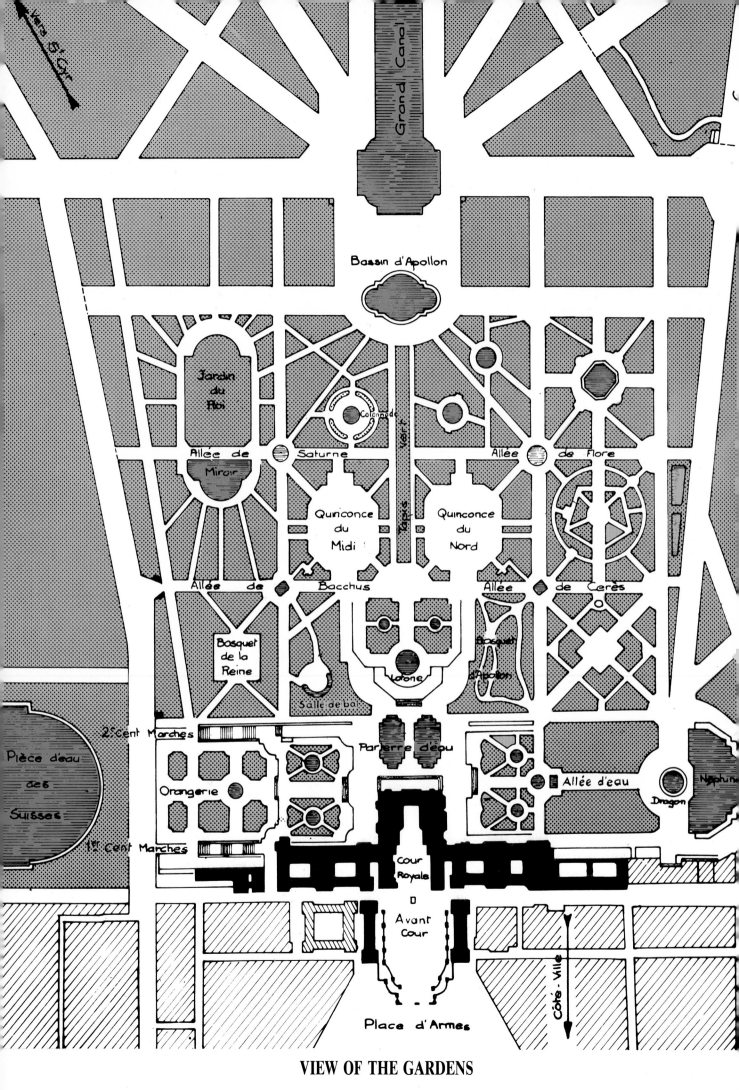

VIEW OF THE GARDENS

THE GARDENS

Nobody would dream of disagreeing with Mademoiselle de Scudéry, who said: "It is most certainly the variety of the gardens and of the groves which make Versailles so beautiful, for one can find in them all that renders a place agreeable".

After the Tuileries and Vaux-le-Vicomte, le Nôtre designed a large part of the Versailles gardens. His task was far from easy, as he had to subdue the unfavourable natural surrounding of the Château. Out of the 6000 ha (14,826 acres) of the Grand Park, he took 1700 (4190) to lay out the large perspective of the Small Park (extending from the Galie farm to the *Pièce d'Eau de Suisse*). It is however in the 95 ha (235 acres) of the gardens that he gave full measure of his genius, combined with that of Le Brun and of the Italian sculptors and forestry experts (the Francines). The splendour of the terraces, the ramps, the lakes, the stairs flanked by tall arbours, the fountain sheltering groves, the bronze or lead decorated

ponds reached its peak during the entertainments given by Louis XIV for Mademoiselle de Lavallière (1664) and Madame de Montespan (1668). These celebrations included theatre plays (Molière), music (Lully), decorations (Le Brun), fireworks and dancing waters (Vigarani).

Being an open-air man, Louis XIV loved the harmony of the creation so much, that he wrote a "Manner of Presenting the Gardens of Versailles", commissioned a series of "views of the gardens", now displayed in the "Cotelle Gallery" in the Trianon, and had a "wheelchair" built so as to be able to go for a ride in the gardens when he suffered from some gout attack. He spared no expense to bring water up to his fountains and ponds (the "Marly machine", the Maintenon aqueduct) and yet he never resigned himself to alternating his dancing waters!

VIEW OF THE GARDENS △   77

On the terrace, under the windows of the War and Peace Drawing-Rooms, the two vases by Coysevox **(War)** and Tubi **(Peace)** stand for the King's victories and the Nimègue peace.

THE PEACE VASE △

The South Parterre

"On leaving the château by the vestibule opening onto the Marble Courtyard, one will reach the terrace; one must then pause at the top of the steps to contemplate the layout of the parterres, ponds and fountains as seen from the Cabinets". Spreading out beneath the windows of the Queen's Apartment, the South Parterre still displays its original design of trimmed box-trees and flower beds, lined with bronze vases. The two sphinx riding Cupids by Lerambert ans Sarrasin belonged to the very first decoration pattern of the Versailles Gardens (1660-1668). The design of the parterre was modified several times: until 1701, it was decorated with the bronze statues (replicas of ancient works) that now stand on the West Terrace. "On reaching the Sphinx, one will pause to behold the South Parterre and then go straight on the top of the Orangery, from where one can see the lines of orange trees and the Lake of the Swiss Guards *(Pièce d'eau des Suisses)*".

The Orangery

The "garden of oranges-trees" should be seen from above (most of it hidden by the parterre it supports) and from the bottom of the Hundred Steps. The building is about 150 m (508 feet) long and maintains a temperature of 6° (42,8°F). In winter, it shelters 1200 orange trees, palm trees, etc., which are brought out in summer. It was constructed by Mansart (1684-1686) to replace the former orangery that Le Vau had built closer to the Château.

Flanked by two monumental staircases ("the Hundred Steps"), it supports an immense platform on which the South Wing was built to house the Princes' apartments. Its parterre is made up of lawn patches and decorated with two *Rapes* (included in the Great Commission of 1674): **Saturn Raping Cybele** by Regnaudin and **Boreus Raping Orythia** by Marsy and Flamen, Farther on lies the Lake of the Swiss Guards *(la pièce d'eau des Suisses),* which was dug in 1679 by the Swiss guards in order to drain the ponds and swamps that stretched there.

△ THE ORANGERY   THE ORANGERY, BY MARTIN △

The Water Parterre

The initial layout of the Parterre was to include a pond of intricate design surrounded by marble statues: these statues, commissioned in 1674, were finally used to decorate the North Parterre. The construction was simplified in 1684: at the foot of the Italian façade lie two large ponds bordered with bronze statues representing the rivers of France, which were cast by the Kellers after sculptures by Tuby (**Rhône** and **Saône**), Coysevox (**Garonne** and **Dordogne**), Le Hongre (**Seine** and **Marne**) and Regaudin (**Loire** and **Loiret**). These lying statues echoed the amplitude of Mansart's façade and constituted a national counterpart to the replicas of ancient sculptures on the terrace (**Bacchus, Apollo** of Belvedere, **Mercury, Silenus**). During the same period, Le Brun decorated the Hall of Mirrors, drawing not on antiquity but on the glorious history of Louis XIV's early reign: art was asserting its national existence.

THE WATER PARTERRE △   THE WATER, BY LE GROS ▷

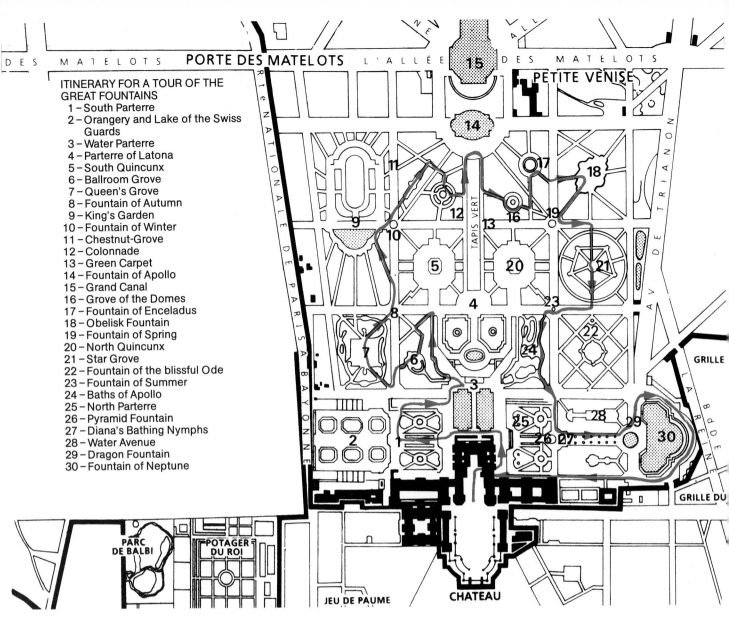

ITINERARY FOR A TOUR OF THE GREAT FOUNTAINS

1 – South Parterre
2 – Orangery and Lake of the Swiss Guards
3 – Water Parterre
4 – Parterre of Latona
5 – South Quincunx
6 – Ballroom Grove
7 – Queen's Grove
8 – Fountain of Autumn
9 – King's Garden
10 – Fountain of Winter
11 – Chestnut-Grove
12 – Colonnade
13 – Green Carpet
14 – Fountain of Apollo
15 – Grand Canal
16 – Grove of the Domes
17 – Fountain of Enceladus
18 – Obelisk Fountain
19 – Fountain of Spring
20 – North Quincunx
21 – Star Grove
22 – Fountain of the blissful Ode
23 – Fountain of Summer
24 – Baths of Apollo
25 – North Parterre
26 – Pyramid Fountain
27 – Diana's Bathing Nymphs
28 – Water Avenue
29 – Dragon Fountain
30 – Fountain of Neptune

▽ THE FOUNTAIN OF APOLLO

THE FOUNTAIN OF NEPTUNE, BY MARTIN ▷

"One must then continue straight on to the top of the Latona parterre and pause there to contemplate Latona, the lizards, the ramps, the statues, the Royal Avenue, the Fountain of Apollo and the Canal and then look back at the parterre and the château". This is one of the oldest fountains in the park, as its site was already laid out under Louis XIII. This Oval pond was then situated in the middle of the half-moon parterre facing the Château. Soon afterwards, Le Nôtre redesigned it and the Marsy brothers started work on the huge ensemble of marble, lead and brass statues which made up a real landscape and was to illustrate the story of Latona.

The Fountain Plays (Grandes Eaux)

Even though Le Nôtre only visited Italy in a late period of his creation, the pattern of the gardens surrounding the great Roman or Florentine villas was well-known thoughout Europe at the time. In Versailles, however, the land was not steep and the only water came from the marshes. The gardens, therefore, had to be laid out starting from the château (the Italian villa was usually hidden in greenery) and the sound of cascades to be replaced by that of fountains gushing several dozen feet up into the air. But the water consumption was such that a circuit had to be set up so as to open and close the gates as one walked on.

That which the whole of Europe admired then and which the tourist wonders at today was, paradoxically, one of Louis XIV's failures!

The marble statues that had been planned for the Latona Parterre were finally set up on the edge of the North Parterre. The drawings for these sculptures had been made by Lebrun according to a very ambitious programme taken from the Italian Ripa's Iconology. The statues represented the Four Seasons, the Four Continents (Oceania was not yet considered one), the Four Elements (Air, Earth, Water and Fire), the Four Parts of the Day (Dawn, Midday or Venus, Evening or Diana and Night), the Four Temperaments (sanguine, choleric, phlegmatic and melancolic) and the Four Types of Poetry (heroic, pastoral, lyric and satyric).

The two ponds on either side echo the main theme of the Lycian peasants' metamorphosis.

The Fountain of Latona

The general theme of this part of the garden was taken from Apollo's story and this fountain features Latona, Apollo's mother. Pregnant by Jupiter, who loved her, she was chased by Python, Juno's serpent, who never let her rest during her pregnancy. Here, flanked by her children, she begs Jupiter to do her justice, for she has been insulted by the peasants of Lycia; to revenge her and punish the offenders, he turns the latter into lizards and frogs.

△ THE FOUNTAIN OF LATONA

THE FOUNTAIN OF LATONA (DETAIL) ▷

◁ THE METAMORPHOSIS OF THE LYCIANS

The Ballroom or Le Bosquet des Rocailles

"One will reach the Ballroom, walk around it and then go to the middle of it".

Using a natural declivity of the ground, Le Nôtre built an amphitheatre "ballroom" (1681-83). Seventeen cascades gush out of the tiers and flow down on the rockwork decorated with Madagascar and Red Sea shells and interspersed with Languedoc marble gullets. The central marble platform was used by the dancers; the musicians stood above the cascade. The large gilded candlestands by Le Gros, Jouvent, etc. would hold crystal candelabra to "light this ballroom at night".

THE BALLROOM GROVE ▷

The Quincunes

In 1663, when Le Nôtre started work on the gardens, the sites of the South and North Quincunes were respectively marked by the Candelabra Grove *(la Girandole)* and the Dauphin Grove. The two groves were replaced by Quincunes during the great changes that Louis XVI ordered at the beginning of his reign. While resting in the shade of the trees, one cannot help contemplating the marble terms made after Poussin's drawings, which Fouquet had commissioned for Vaux-le-Vicomte in 1665 and sold to Louis XIV in 1683.

The Queen's Grove

This setting is an example of the "bucolic" taste of the late 18th century. It was designed by Hubert Robert in 1775 to replace the Labyrinth, one of Le Nôtre's most sumptuous groves, made up of "an infinite number of narrow paths, so intricate that it is almost impossible not to lose one's way in there" (Ch. Perrault). Built in 1673, the Labyrinth had 39 fountains, each decorated with lead sculptures painted in natural tones and representing themes from Aesop's fables. They had an educational purpose, being meant to illustrate the fables for Monseigneur (the Dauphin, Louis XIV's son), whose tutor was Bossuet. Each fountain was therefore completed with a moral by Benserade in the same way in which La Fontaine ended up his fables. One can get an idea of that fanciful setting by contemplating the life like animal statues that remain or, better still, the paintings made by Cotelle for the Trianon gallery in 1688.

△ THE SOUTH QUINCUNES

THE QUEEN'S GROVE ▷

86

The Fountains of the Seasons

Running parallel to the Grand Perspective, which stretches from the Water Parterre to the Grand Canal, are the secondary axes designed by Le Nôtre. The two main ones are marked by the Season Fountains: The *Fountain of Autumn* by the Marsy brothers and the *Fountain of Winter* by Girardon to the South; the *Fountain of Summer* by Regnaudin and the *Fountain of Spring* by Tuby, symmetrically to the North.

THE FOUNTAIN OF AUTUMN ▷

The Colonnade

"One will enter the Colonnade, walk to the middle of it, then walk around to contemplate the columns, the arches, the low-reliefs and the basins. On leaving, one must pause to behold Guidy's group". This colonnade designed by Mansart replaced the former *Parterre des Sources* by Le Nôtre and was a usual setting for suppers and light refreshments. It also proved "that marble is nowadays more common in France than in Italy". The arches are supported by couples of columns and pilasters made of polychrome marble (slate blue, violet breccia, Languedoc). The tympans are decorated with reliefs depicting music playing Cupids while the voussoirs are made up of nymph, naïad and sylvan heads. The light and extremly elegant sculptures are the work of a particulary brilliant team of artists (Tuby, Le Hongre, Coysevox, Van Cleve) and foreshadow the decorative style of the Chapel. In 1699, Louis XIV had *The Rape of Persephone* by Girardon placed there; this statue has been sheltered in the *Grande Ecurie*.

The Green Carpet (Tapis Vert)

This 335 m (1 100 feet) long "Royal avenue" stretches between the two ponds dedicated to Apollo: from her fountain, Latona gazes, as it were, towards her son who is driving away on his chariot. The avenue is lined with vases and statues. Unlike the statues, most of which are replicas of ancient sculptures, the vases display decorative patterns typical of Versailles: sunflowers, fleur-de-lis, cornucopias, laurel and oak leaves evocative of the Royal virtues and bounty. These works were made by the students of the Academy of France in Rome.

△ THE FOUNTAIN OF WINTER

THE ROYAL AVENUE OR THE GREEN CARPET ▷

While the château was being enlarged eastwards, with annexes that spread out into the town itself, the gardens thickened and expanded into the opposite direction. The relatively simple pattern of large squares on either side of the great axis grew ever more intricate, which even affected the perspective choices. The challenge was no longer that of subduing nature but of blending it with art: foliages coupled with marbles, whether iconographic or decorative; the façade overlooking the lying bronze statues, which enhanced the magic of the light outlining the planes; shady groves sheltering the gilded or polychrome lead statues that echo the sound of water.

THE COLONNADE △

89

Cyparissus, the Shepherd

Legend has it that Cyparissus was the young shepherd who fed the stag consecrated to the nymphs of Carthaea. The stag's horns glittered like gold and his forehead was ornated with a silver globe. Chains of precious stones were hanging on his breast and his ears were adorned with pearls swinging down to his hollow temples. He was not in the least wild: Cyparissus would ride him to the water and put chains of flowers around his neck. One day, the tired stag lay down in the shade and Cyparissus accidentally pierced him dead with his javelin. He was so overwhelmed with grief that he begged Apollo to let him mourn eternally. When he had wept out all his blood, his limbs turned green and his hair stood on end. Apollo then told him: "I will shed tears on you and you will shed tears on the others. You will be the companion of grief". Such is the symbolical meaning of the cypress.

△ CYPARISSUS, THE SHEPHERD, BY FLAMEN

THE FOUNTAIN OF APOLLO △

The Fountain of Apollo

Under Louis XIII a pond was dug here (1639) which became known as the "Pond of the Swans". When Louis XIV had it enlarged (1671), Le Brun suggested that it should be dedicated to Apollo. For even if Versailles was not meant as a temple to the Sun God its East-West orientation and the commonly drawn parallel between the King and Apollo prompted the artists to elaborate on the Sun iconography. Le Brun's Apollo, sitting on his chariot drawn by four fiery horses, is just emerging from the ocean surrounding the Grotto of Thetys where he has spent the night. This dawn theme had already been superbly illustrated in the ceiling paintings of some Italian palaces (Guido Reni in the Rospigliosi Palace and Guerchini in the Ludovisi Palace) and had given its name to the most beautiful of the Louvre's galleries (La Fose's decoration of what was to became the Throne Room).

Looking towards the Château, Latona and the Grotto of Thetys, Apollo is not standing, as an ancient chariot driver would: he is sitting calmly, as if to control his horses better. This gilded sculpture was made by Tuby, a native of Rome, and was installed in 1671. Beyond the fountain lies the Grand Canal on which Louis XIV had a flotilla sail, both as a symbol of the Royal Navy and as a means of transport to the Trianon.

ARISTEUS AND PROTEUS, BY SLODTZ ▷

The Obelisk

The tour of the Great Fountains enables the visitor to contemplate all the aspects of the Versailles fountains: baroque and musical as in the Rockwork Grove *(des Rocailles)* or impressively turbulent as in the Apollo pond, which stands in striking contrast to the 1 500 m (5 118 feet) long and 120 m (394 feet) wide Canal. The fountains hidden in the groves or under the trees are a reserve of surprises: Marsy portrays Enceladus, buried under a mass of rocks, in a pathetic effort to tear himself free; the Fountain of the Domes, on the other hand, is all serenity (even though it was altered many times) and echoes the resting attitude of Apollo and his horses, which stood here for a while. Finally the Obelisk Fountain, former Banquet Hall, is made up of water and greenery, with a clump of reeds from which more than 200 jets spring: Mansart, who built it in 1706, did not make use of any decorative effects.

THE FOUNTAIN OF THE CHILDREN'S ISLAND △

◁ THE OBELISK FOUNTAIN

The North Parterre

In contrast with the South Parterre, to which it is symmetrical, the North Parterre slopes gently down to the Dragon Fountain. Among the finest works are the Crown Fountains, with their playful tritons, and Girardon's **Bathing Nymphs** which overhang the slope and the sites of two former groves: the Triumphal Arch and the Three Fountains. Besides the "great commission" of 1674, the North Parterre also displays the Ancient Philpsopher's Roundabout on the upper side of the Apollo Baths.

GENERAL VIEW
OF THE NORTH PARTERRE ▷

93

The Water Avenue

"One will walk along the Children's avenue".

The avenue slopes gently down from the Bathing Nymphs to the Dragon and was apparently conceived by Charles Perrault. The statues of the children *(les marmousets)* were sculpted by Buirette, Le Hongre, Lerambert and Mazeline after Le Brun's drawings. At the beginning (1670), they were made of gilt lead with flower and fruit baskets painted in natural tones. In 1688, the whole was cast in bronze.

THE WATER AVENUE ▷

The Pyramid Fountain

This fountain was designed by Le Brun and executed by Girardon in 1679. It was originally gilded and is exclusively decorated with aquatic beings: shellfish, dolphins and tritons.

△ THE NORTH PARTERRE

THE PYRAMID FOUNTAIN △

The Dragon Fountain and the Fountain Neptune

"One will turn around the Dragon and contemplate the jets and the statue of Neptune."

This is where the tour of the Great Fountains ends today. The first reason for that it technical: however magnificient the performance, it is a real feat and it requires all the other fountain plays to stop for the Dragon to be able to spurt out its 27 m (90 feet) jet. Under Louis XIV, the high jet was let out only in the presence of the King; otherwise it was lowered to 11 m (35 feet). The dragon fought down by swan-riding children was executed by Marsy (1687) and was so badly damaged by the 19th century that it had to be replaced.

Planned by Le Nôtre in 1679, the Fountain of Neptune ends, to the North, the perspective of the Parterre and of the Water Avenue closed off by Guidi's statue **The King's Fame** (counterpart of Bernini's **Marcus Curtius** which overhung, until recently, the *Pièce d'eau des suisses* to the South). This vast statuary was only completed in 1738, by Gabriel. Its great number of jets (almost one hundred in all) make it the most imposing fountain in the Versailles gardens. The sculptures decorating it include lead vases, sea cupids and, naturally, the three central groups: **Neptune and Amphitrite** (L.A. Adam), **Proteus**, Neptune's son (Bouchardon) and the **Ocean** (Lemoine). The fountain was inaugurated by Louis XV in 1741.

△ THE FOUNTAIN OF NEPTUNE (DETAIL)

96

THE FOUNTAIN OF NEPTUNE △

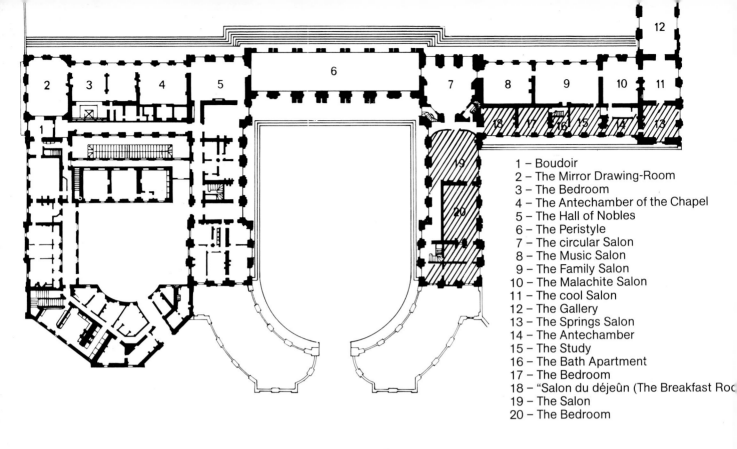

1 – Boudoir
2 – The Mirror Drawing-Room
3 – The Bedroom
4 – The Antechamber of the Chapel
5 – The Hall of Nobles
6 – The Peristyle
7 – The circular Salon
8 – The Music Salon
9 – The Family Salon
10 – The Malachite Salon
11 – The cool Salon
12 – The Gallery
13 – The Springs Salon
14 – The Antechamber
15 – The Study
16 – The Bath Apartment
17 – The Bedroom
18 – "Salon du déjeûn (The Breakfast Roo
19 – The Salon
20 – The Bedroom

TRIANON

The Grand Trianon

Trianon was the name of a village bought by Louis XIV to enlarge his domain. He very soon embellished it by building a pavilion that was adorned with white and blue China tiles and was therefore known us the Porcelain Trianon. Unfortunately, this Trianon soon started deteriorating, its tiles came off and it finally fell into ruin. In 1687, Mansart erected the present château, called the Marble Trianon. After its recent restoration (1965), the paintings commissioned by Louis XV were brought back to the Trianon and so was most of the furniture commissioned by Napoleon, who stayed there with Empress Marie-Louise. In the **Mirror Cabinet**, the visitor can admire the view of the gardens and of the Grand Canal as well as Marie-Louise's pianoforte and the table-center offered by Charles IV. The bed in the **King's Bedchamber** is Napoleon's bed in the Tuileries. On the other side of the peristyle (created at Louis XIV's suggestion) lies the **Grand Drawing Room**, where one can see the large "family tables" on which Queen Marie-Amélie and her daughters used to put away their fancy work. Next to it the **Malachite Drawing-Room**, so called because of the stones offered by Tsar Alexander I to Napoleon is decorated with 24 paintings representing the gardens under Louis XIV. Its pictorial decoration recalls that the Trianon is surrounded by magnificent gardens, where the flowers would sometimes be changed every day.

△ THE MIRROR CABINET

◁ THE GRAND TRIANON, BY MARTIN

THE KING'S BEDCHAMBER △

The Trianon Gardens

The gardens were designed by Le Bouteux and Le Nôtre for the Porcelain Trianon and were enlarged by Mansart. One can come from the peristyle straight into the Upper Garden, made up of parterres and ponds. From the Lower Garden one can see the Grand Canal stretching to the left; straigth ahead, the eye is caught by the **Platfond,** by Hardy's dragons, children, shellfish and reeds which adorn three superposed layers as well as by Mansart's cascade. Between the Costelle Gallery and the Trianon-sous-Bois wing lies the former Garden of the Spring **(Jardin des Sources)** where "small canals winding randomly... fall into empty spaces with unevenly placed jets.". **The King's Garden** looks just as it did under Louis XIV and Madame de Maintenon; "it is always full of flowers that are changed every season... More than a million pots of flowers have to be continually changed, taken out, carried and brought back". The smell of tuberoses was sometimes so strong that the Court could not stay there long.

THE GALLERY OF ANTIQUES, BY MARTIN △

▷ THE PERISTYLE

◁ THE GARDEN DRAWING-ROOM

The Emperor at Trianon

Napoleon, who was first and foremost concerned with renovating the Château of Versailles (the silk hangings he had commissioned for that purpose have been preserved), occupied the right wing and fore-wing for a while. The rooms where he worked or lived his family life have been readorned with the beautiful furniture by Jacob and Marcion, the bronzes by Thomire and, of course, the allegorical paintings commissioned by Louis XIV.

△ THE GARDEN FACADE OF THE TRIANON PALACE

THE EMPEROR'S BEDCHAMBER △

The Small Trianon

Louis XV commissioned Richard to create a botanical garden where coffee trees, fig trees and ananases were grown. He also had Gabriel build a château (1763-68), which Louis XVI was to give to Marie-Antoinette. The latter asked Mique to turn the place into an English garden, dotted with "fabrics". The château was built on a square ground plan and is made up of a ground level, a first storey and an attic surrounded by a balustrade, where Louis XV's apartment was.

◁ THE SMALL TRIANON

THE TEMPLE OF LOVE ▽

△ THE RECEPTION ROOM

THE BELVEDERE ▷

102